800 ENGLISH IDIOMS FROM
I - P

MASTER COMMON EXPRESSIONS FOR FLUENCY AND CONFIDENT COMMUNICATION FOR INTERMEDIATE AND ADVANCED LEARNERS

IDIOMS
BOOK TWO

A M LUCAS

INTRODUCTION

ENGLISH IDIOMS

If grammar is the skeleton of a language and vocabulary represents the blood vessels, then idioms are the meat of the English language. Idioms (in any language) give a language luster, shine, and poetry.

Mastering idioms is not just about adding to your vocabulary. It's about transforming your language skills from basic to intermediate or advanced. Idioms are the key to expressing yourself with eloquence and sophistication.

They add color to descriptions and phraseology in your sentences; they add life and excitement; through them, you can tell stories, and your narratives become much better.

So, let's go through the idioms of the English language, starting from A—Z. This book deals with idioms starting from I—P. It is the second book in a three-part series alphabetically outlining the idioms. Of course, there are too many, so we will choose the more popular ones.

THE RULES OF IDIOMS

The rules of idioms are that they are rigid. You have to use it in its exact form except unless a verb is attached to an idiom, in which case subject-verb agreement comes into play.

E.g., the idiom *"take sides"*. The word take is a verb.

So you say: *She takes side* with her father while her *sisters take sides* with their mother.

This is only when the idiom starts with a verb. For those of you not in the know, a verb is an action word that requires doing.

Other than that, an idiom is a rigid phrase. You cannot change any word in that phrase.

Example:

Idiom: Apple of somebody's eye

Correct: She is the *apple of her mother's eye.*

It cannot be changed to:

Incorrect: She is the *apple of her mother's eyes.*

Another example:

Idiom: All thumbs

Correct: He was *all thumbs* when it came to carpentry, but he was great at sewing.

Incorrect: He was *all thumb* when it came to carpentry, but he was great at sewing

Incorrect: He was *all fingers* when it came to carpentry, but he was great at sewing

Incorrect: He was *all the thumbs* when it came to carpentry, but he was great at sewing

You must follow the rule strictly: do not change the idiom except when it comes to subject-verb agreement and keeping in line with the tenses.

Example:

Idiom: wash one's dirty linen in public

Correct: She *washed her dirty linen in public* much to her family's horror.

Incorrect: She *wash her dirty linen in public* much to her family's horror.

Incorrect: She *washed her dirty linens in public* much to her family's horror.

Correct: They are in the habit of *washing their dirty linen in public.*

Incorrect: They are in the habit of <u>*wash*</u> their dirty linen in public.

Incorrect: They are in the habit of *washing their dirty linen in <u>the</u> public.*

SO ONCE AGAIN, THERE ARE TWO MAIN RULES:

Do not change the form of the idiom in any way except in two instances:

1. When the idiom begins with a verb, and you have to apply the rules of subject-verb agreement

2. When you have to apply the tenses when the idiom starts with a verb

THE WAY TO LEARN IDIOMS

1. A good way to learn idioms is to say the idiom aloud (you have to hear it tripping off your tongue).

2. And then repeat it three times.

3. Again, if sample sentences are given, repeat them three times.

A GOOD WAY TO START:

1 Look through the list of idioms and tick the ones that you are familiar with. This will give you more confidence as a language learner.

2 Next, look at the examples given of the ones that you are familiar with and note usage.

3 Write a simple sentence using the idiom. This will help you memorize and familiarise yourself with it.

4 When you look at the rest of the idioms you have not ticked, these will denote idioms you are not familiar with. Decide whether they will be useful in the context of your life situation, and then choose to memorize them or not. This way, you may not be overwhelmed by the plethora of idioms in the English language.

5 This book is written for older learners of English, and the idioms chosen are for working adults. So, if an idiom is relevant to your workplace, it's a good place to start. This way, you may not be overwhelmed by the plethora of idioms in the English language.

6 Do remember to have fun along the way. Some idioms don't make literal sense, but if you look for the metaphor, it makes sense! Laugh throughout this learning journey.

ACTIVITIES AT THE END OF EACH CHAPTER

The activities at the end of the chapters are also tailored towards working adults. They can be interactive resources to help you see how often idioms are used in everyday speech. These activities give you more opportunities to learn how to use the idioms within the right context. The answer keys are given in Chapter 9.

WITH THESE POINTS IN MIND, LET'S BEGIN.

IDIOMS BEGINNING WITH I

*H*ere's the 100

1 ICING ON THE CAKE

Meaning: An additional benefit.

Example: Winning the award was the icing on the cake.

Example: The sunny weather was the icing on the cake for their trip.

2 IDLE MINDS ARE THE DEVIL'S WORKSHOP

Meaning: Having nothing to do leads to trouble.

Example: He believes that idle minds are the devil's workshop.

Example: They kept the children busy, knowing that idle minds are the devil's workshop.

Idle minds are the devil's workshop

3 IF THE CAP FITS, WEAR IT

Meaning: Accept a description if it applies to you.

Example: If the cap fits, wear it; you know you're responsible.

Example: She told him, "If the cap fits, wear it," when he denied his faults.

4 IF THE SHOE FITS, WEAR IT

Meaning: If a description applies to you, accept it.

Example: He said he wasn't a good listener, and she replied, "If the shoe fits, wear it."

Example: If the shoe fits, wear it; don't deny your faults.

5 IF WISHES WERE HORSES, BEGGARS WOULD RIDE

Meaning: Merely wishing for something won't make it happen.

Example: He said, "If wishes were horses, beggars would ride," when she talked about her dreams.

Example: If wishes were horses, beggars would ride, so you need to work hard to achieve your goals.

6 IGNORANCE IS BLISS

Meaning: Not knowing something is often more comfortable than knowing it.

Example: Sometimes ignorance is bliss, especially when it comes to bad news.

Example: She chose not to read the negative reviews, believing ignorance is bliss.

7 ILL AT EASE

Meaning: Uncomfortable or uneasy.

Example: He felt ill at ease in the formal attire.

Example: She was ill at ease during the job interview.

8 ILL EFFECTS

Meaning: Negative consequences or results.

Example: The medication caused some ill effects, including dizziness.

Example: The pollution had several ill effects on the environment.

9 ILL FEELING

Meaning: Resentment or animosity.

Example: There was ill feeling between the neighbors after the dispute.

Example: The argument left a lot of ill feeling between them.

10 ILL WILL

Meaning: Hostility or animosity.

Example: There was ill will between the two rival companies.

Example: Despite their differences, he held no ill will towards her.

11 ILL-ADVISED

Meaning: Not wise or sensible; badly thought out.

Example: His decision to quit his job without another offer was ill-advised.

Example: The company made an ill-advised investment in the failing market.

12 ILL-ASSORTED

Meaning: Poorly matched or not suited to each other.

Example: The ill-assorted couple argued constantly.

Example: The ill-assorted furniture made the room look chaotic.

13 ILL-BRED

Meaning: Rude or poorly behaved.

Example: His ill-bred comments offended everyone at the dinner.

Example: She found his ill-bred behavior unacceptable.

14 ILL-CONCEIVED

Meaning: Poorly planned or thought out.

Example: The ill-conceived project was doomed from the start.

Example: Their ill-conceived plan quickly fell apart.

15 ILL-DISPOSED

Meaning: Unfriendly or having a negative attitude.

Example: He was ill-disposed towards the new policies.

Example: She was ill-disposed to help after their argument.

16 ILL-EQUIPPED

Meaning: Not having the necessary equipment or skills.

Example: The team was ill-equipped to handle the emergency.

Example: She felt ill-equipped for the new job responsibilities.

17 ILL-FATED

Meaning: Destined to fail or have bad luck.

Example: The ill-fated voyage ended in disaster.

Example: Their ill-fated business venture cost them a lot of money.

18 ILL-FITTING

Meaning: Not fitting properly.

Example: He wore an ill-fitting suit to the interview.

Example: The ill-fitting shoes gave her blisters.

19 ILL-FOUNDED

Meaning: Not based on fact or reliable evidence.

Example: His accusations were ill-founded and unfair.

Example: The rumors about the company's bankruptcy were ill-founded.

20 ILL-GOTTEN GAINS

Meaning: Money or benefits obtained illegally or unethically.

Example: He was arrested for his ill-gotten gains.

Example: She felt guilty about her ill-gotten gains.

21 ILL-JUDGED

Meaning: Poorly thought out or unwise.

Example: His ill-judged remarks upset many people.

Example: The company's ill-judged decision led to financial losses.

22 ILL-MANNERED

Meaning: Rude or impolite.

Example: His ill-mannered behavior embarrassed his parents.

Example: She was shocked by his ill-mannered response.

23 ILL-PREPARED

Meaning: Not ready or inadequately prepared.

Example: The team was ill-prepared for the competition.

Example: She felt ill-prepared for the exam.

24 ILL-TIMED

Meaning: Happening at an inappropriate or inconvenient time.

Example: His joke was ill-timed and offended many people.

Example: The ill-timed announcement caused confusion.

25 ILL-TREATMENT

Meaning: Harsh or cruel treatment.

Example: The prisoners complained about their ill-treatment.

Example: She suffered ill treatment at the hands of her employer.

26 IMITATION IS THE SINCEREST FORM OF FLATTERY

Meaning: Copying someone is a way of paying them a compliment.

Example: When her little sister started dressing like her, she realized that imitation is the sincerest form of flattery.

Example: He didn't mind the plagiarism, believing imitation is the sincerest form of flattery.

27 IMMEDIATELY OBVIOUS

Meaning: Clear or apparent without delay.

Example: The solution was immediately obvious to her.

Example: The mistake was immediately obvious when we reviewed the work.

28 IMMERSE SOMEBODY/SOMETHING IN SOMETHING

Meaning: To involve someone or something deeply in an activity or interest.

Example: She immersed herself in her studies to avoid thinking about the breakup.

Example: They immersed the fabric in dye to achieve a deep color.

29 IMPART SOMETHING TO SOMEBODY

Meaning: To give or communicate something to someone.

Example: The teacher imparted valuable knowledge to her students.

Example: He imparted his wisdom to the younger generation.

30 IMPATIENT TO DO SOMETHING

Meaning: Eager and unable to wait to do something.

Example: She was impatient to open her birthday presents.

Example: He grew impatient to start the project.

31 IMPENDING DISASTER/DANGER/DOOM

Meaning: A situation that is likely to lead to significant trouble, catastrophe, or failure in the near future.

Example: The engineers warned of an impending disaster if the dam was not reinforced before the rainy season.

Example: The company's financial reports indicated impending doom, leading to panic among the investors.

32 IMPLICATION OF SOMEBODY IN SOMETHING

Meaning: The involvement or connection of someone in an event or situation, often suggesting wrongdoing or responsibility.

Example: The implication of the manager in the scandal shocked the entire company.

Example: His implication in the crime was confirmed by the evidence.

33 IMPOSSIBLE DREAM

Meaning: A goal or aspiration that seems unattainable or unrealistic, often because it is so ambitious or difficult to achieve.

Example: Despite facing numerous setbacks, Marie refused to give up on what others called her *impossible dream* of becoming a world-renowned author.

Example: Climbing Mount Everest was once considered an *impossible dream*, but hundreds of adventurers now attempt the feat yearly.

34 IMPREGNATE SOMEBODY WITH SOMETHING

Meaning: To fill someone or something with a particular quality or feeling.

Example: The teacher tried to impregnate her students with a love for reading.

Example: The room was impregnated with the smell of fresh flowers.

35 IMPRESS SOMEBODY WITH SOMETHING

Meaning: To make someone admire or respect something you do or have.

Example: She impressed the interviewers with her extensive knowledge of the subject.

Example: He impressed his friends with his cooking skills.

36 IMPRINT SOMETHING ON YOUR MIND/MEMORY/BRAIN

Meaning: To make a lasting impression or memory.

Example: The tragic event was imprinted on her mind forever.

Example: He imprinted the important dates on his memory.

37 IMPULSE BUYING/SHOPPING

Meaning: Purchasing items without prior planning or consideration.

Example: She regretted her impulse buying after seeing her credit card bill.

Example: Impulse shopping can lead to unnecessary expenses.

38 IMPULSE TO DO SOMETHING

Meaning: A sudden strong desire to act.

Example: She had an impulse to call her friend late at night.

Example: He felt an impulse to quit his job and travel the world.

39 IN A BIND

Meaning: In a difficult situation.

Example: He found himself in a bind when his car broke down.

Example: She's in a bind because she has two deadlines to meet.

40 IN A FLASH

Meaning: Very quickly.

Example: The meeting ended in a flash.

Example: She finished her homework in a flash.

41 IN A HEARTBEAT

Meaning: Very quickly; without hesitation.

Example: I'd move to New York in a heartbeat if I had the chance.

Example: He said he would quit his job in a heartbeat for a better offer.

42 IN A HUFF

Meaning: In an annoyed or angry state.

Example: She left the meeting in a huff when her ideas were rejected.

Example: He walked away in a huff after the argument.

43 IN A JAM

Meaning: In a difficult situation.

Example: He's in a jam because he lost his wallet.

Example: She found herself in a jam when her car broke down.

44 IN A JIFFY

Meaning: Very quickly.

Example: I'll be back in a jiffy.

Example: She finished the task in a jiffy.

45 IN A LATHER

Meaning: In a state of agitation or excitement.

Example: He was in a lather about the meeting.

Example: She got in a lather over the smallest things.

46 IN A NUTSHELL

Meaning: In a brief summary.

Example: In a nutshell, the project was a success.

Example: He explained the plan in a nutshell.

47 IN A PICKLE

Meaning: In a difficult situation.

Example: I'm in a pickle because I forgot my wallet.

Example: She's in a pickle, trying to balance work and family life.

48 IN A RUT

Meaning: Stuck in a monotonous routine.

Example: He feels like he's in a rut at his job.

Example: They decided to travel to get out of their rut.

49 IN A TIGHT SPOT

Meaning: In a difficult situation.

Example: She's in a tight spot with her finances.

Example: He found himself in a tight spot after losing his job.

50 IN ALL HONESTY

Meaning: To speak truthfully.

Example: In all honesty, I didn't like the movie.

Example: She told him, in all honesty, that she wasn't interested.

51 IN AN IMPOSSIBLE POSITION

Meaning: In a situation where it is very difficult to act or decide.

Example: He found himself in an impossible position, having to choose between his job and his family.

Example: The manager was in an impossible position, trying to satisfy both the employees and the upper management.

52 IN AN INSTANT

Meaning: Very quickly.

Example: The decision was made in an instant.

Example: She knew in an instant that he was the one.

53 IN BLACK AND WHITE

Meaning: In written form.

Example: We need to get the agreement in black and white.

Example: She prefers to see things in black and white.

54 IN BROAD DAYLIGHT

Meaning: In plain sight, during the day.

Example: The theft occurred in broad daylight.

Example: They argued in broad daylight for everyone to see.

55 IN COLD BLOOD

Meaning: Without emotion or pity; ruthlessly.

Example: The crime was committed in cold blood.

Example: He was accused of lying in cold blood.

56 IN DEEP WATER

Meaning: In trouble or difficulty.

Example: He's in deep water with his debts.

Example: She found herself in deep water after the mistake.

57 IN HOT WATER

Meaning: In trouble or difficulty.

Example: He got into hot water for missing the meeting.

Example: She's in hot water with her boss.

58 IN OVER ONE'S HEAD

Meaning: Involved in something beyond one's ability.

Example: He was in over his head with the new project.

Example: She's in over her head trying to manage everything.

59 IN PLAIN ENGLISH

Meaning: In simple, clear language.

Example: Please explain the instructions in plain English.

Example: He told her the news in plain English.

60 IN SOMEBODY'S IMAGINATION

Meaning: Existing only in someone's mind.

Example: The monster under the bed is just in your imagination.

Example: The idea of a perfect world exists only in someone's imagination.

61 IN SOMEONE'S BAD BOOKS

Meaning: Out of favor with someone.

Example: He's in the boss's bad books for missing the deadline.

Example: She didn't want to be in her friend's bad books.

62 IN SOMEONE'S GOOD BOOKS

Meaning: In favor with someone.

Example: He did extra work to get in the boss's good books.

Example: She's trying to get back in her friend's good books.

63 IN THE BAG

Meaning: Certain to be won or achieved.

Example: With that last goal, the game is in the bag.

Example: She felt the job was in the bag after the interview.

64 IN THE BLINK OF AN EYE

Meaning: Very quickly.

Example: The storm passed in the blink of an eye.

Example: He finished the project in the blink of an eye.

65 IN THE DOGHOUSE

Meaning: In trouble or disfavor.

Example: He's in the doghouse for forgetting their anniversary.

Example: She was in the doghouse after missing the meeting.

66 IN THE DRIVER'S SEAT

Meaning: In control.

Example: She's in the driver's seat on this project.

Example: He likes being in the driver's seat in his career.

67 IN THE HEAT OF THE MOMENT

Meaning: During a moment of heightened emotion.

Example: He said some things he didn't mean in the heat of the moment.

Example: They made a decision in the heat of the moment.

68 IN THE IMAGE OF SOMEBODY

Meaning: Resembling someone closely.

Example: He was created in the image of his father.

Example: The new sculpture is in the image of the ancient Greek gods.

69 IN THE LOOP

Meaning: Informed and up-to-date.

Example: Make sure to keep me in the loop about the project.

Example: He's always in the loop on company decisions.

70 IN THE NICK OF TIME

Meaning: Just in time.

Example: They arrived in the nick of time to catch the train.

Example: She completed the assignment in the nick of time.

71 IN THE SAME BOAT

Meaning: In the same situation.

Example: We're all in the same boat

72 IN THE SPOTLIGHT

Meaning: Receiving a lot of attention.

Example: She doesn't like being in the spotlight.

Example: The new product is in the spotlight this month.

73 IN THE THICK OF IT

Meaning: In the most active or intense part of something.

Example: She was in the thick of it during the crisis.

Example: He's always in the thick of it at work.

74 IN THE WORKS

Meaning: Being planned or developed.

Example: There's a new project in the works.

Example: She has a few ideas in the works.

75 IN THEIR HUNDREDS/THOUSANDS

Meaning: In large numbers.

Example: The fans came to the concert in their thousands.

Example: The protesters gathered in their hundreds outside the government building.

76 IN TWO HALVES/TWO PIECES

Meaning: Divided into two equal or nearly equal parts.

Example: He broke the cookie in two halves and shared it with his sister.

Example: The glass shattered into two pieces when it fell.

77 IN TWO MINDS

Meaning: Undecided about something.

Example: He's in two minds about accepting the job offer.

Example: She's in two minds about moving to a new city.

78 IN YOUR FACE

Meaning: Aggressively confrontational.

Example: His in-your-face attitude annoyed many people.

Example: She doesn't like his in-your-face style of arguing.

79 INCAPABLE OF DOING SOMETHING

Meaning: Lacking the ability or capacity to perform a specific action.

Example: He felt incapable of solving the complex math problem.

Example: She was incapable of hiding her emotions during the argument.

80 INCENTIVE TO DO SOMETHING

Meaning: A reason or motivation to perform a specific action.

Example: The company offered a bonus as an incentive to increase productivity.

Example: The possibility of a promotion was a strong incentive for her to work harder.

81 INCH BY INCH

Meaning: Gradually or slowly, often used to describe a process that takes a long time or requires a lot of effort.

Example: The team worked inch by inch to complete the renovation, ensuring every detail was perfect.

Example: He climbed the mountain inch by inch, taking breaks to catch his breath and enjoy the view.

82 INCISIVE REMARKS/CRITICISM

Meaning: Sharp and clear comments or critiques that are insightful and direct.

Example: His incisive remarks during the meeting clarified the key issues.

Example: The reviewer's incisive criticism of the novel highlighted its weaknesses.

83 INCLINATION TO DO SOMETHING

Meaning: A tendency or natural urge to act or feel in a particular way.

Example: His inclination to do something creative led him to pursue a career in art.

Example: She has an inclination to help others, often volunteering at the local shelter.

84 INCLINED TO AGREE

Meaning: Likely or willing to agree with someone or something.

Example: I am inclined to agree with your opinion on this matter.

Example: She was inclined to agree with the proposed changes after hearing the arguments.

85 INCLINED TO DO SOMETHING

Meaning: Likely or disposed to perform a particular action.

Example: He is inclined to take risks when making investments.

Example: She is inclined to help others whenever she can.

86 INCRIMINATE YOURSELF

Meaning: To make yourself appear guilty of a crime or wrongdoing.

Example: He refused to answer the question to avoid incriminating himself.

Example: Be careful not to incriminate yourself when discussing the incident with the police.

87 INDOMITABLE SPIRIT/COURAGE/WILL

Meaning: A strong, unyielding determination and resilience that cannot be overcome.

Example: Despite her many challenges, her indomitable spirit kept her going.

Example: His indomitable courage in danger inspired everyone around him.

Example: They admired his indomitable will to succeed against all odds.

88 INDUCE SOMEBODY TO DO SOMETHING

Meaning: To persuade or influence someone to take a specific action.

Example: The advertisement was designed to induce people to buy the product.

Example: She induced him to join the club with promises of fun activities.

89 INDULGE YOURSELF

Meaning: To allow yourself to enjoy something special or pleasurable.

Example: After a long week, she indulged herself in a spa day.

Example: He indulged himself in a lavish dinner to celebrate his promotion.

90 INFECTIOUS SMILE/ENTHUSIASM

Meaning: A smile or enthusiasm that is so strong it spreads to others.

Example: Her infectious smile brightened everyone's day.

Example: His infectious enthusiasm motivated the entire team.

91 IT IS IMPERATIVE FOR SOMEBODY TO DO SOMETHING

Meaning: It is absolutely necessary or crucial for someone to do something.

Example: It is imperative for students to attend all classes to pass the course.

Example: It is imperative for her to take her medication on time.

92 IT IS IMPROPER TO DO SOMETHING

Meaning: It is not appropriate or suitable to take a certain action.

Example: It is improper to speak loudly in a library.

Example: It is improper to interrupt someone when they are speaking.

93 IT TAKES TWO TO TANGO

Meaning: Both parties are responsible for a situation.

Example: It takes two to tango, so both of them are to blame for the argument.

Example: Remember, it takes two to tango when discussing a conflict.

94 IT'S NOT ROCKET SCIENCE

Meaning: It's not very complicated.

Example: Following this recipe is not rocket science.

Example: Learning to use the new software isn't rocket science.

95 INCULCATE SOMETHING INTO SOMEBODY

Meaning: to instill or teach an idea, habit, or value persistently and repeatedly in someone's mind, often to encourage them to adopt it as a belief or practice.

Example: Parents often try to inculcate good manners into their children from an early age.

Example: The coach worked hard to inculcate a sense of discipline and teamwork into her players.

96 INCUR SOMEBODY'S DISPLEASURE/WRATH/DISAPPROVAL

Meaning: to do something that causes someone to feel displeased, angry, or disapproving toward you.

Example: By failing to meet the project deadline, he incurred his manager's displeasure.

Example: She spoke out of turn during the meeting and incurred the wrath of the senior executives.

97 INDIGNITY OF DOING SOMETHING

Meaning: refers to the feeling of shame, embarrassment, or loss of respect caused by having to perform a particular action, often one that is perceived as humiliating in some way.

Example: He suffered the indignity of being searched in front of his colleagues

Example: The indignity of having to ask for help was almost too much for her pride to bear.

98 INDRAWN BREATH

Meaning: a sharp or sudden intake of breath, usually caused by surprise, shock, fear, or anticipation.

Example: There was an indrawn breath from the audience as the magician performed his final trick.

Example: At the sound of the crash, he drew an indrawn breath, fearing the worst.

99 INDULGE YOURSELF

Meaning: to allow yourself to enjoy a particular pleasure or to give in to a desire, often something that brings comfort, joy, or satisfaction.

Example: After a long week, she decided to indulge herself with a spa day.

Example: Go ahead, indulge yourself with a piece of chocolate cake.

100 INFORMED DECISION/CHOICE/JUDGEMENT

Meaning: refers to a decision, choice, or judgment made with a thorough understanding of all relevant information and factors.

Example: She made an informed decision to invest in the company after reviewing their financial reports.

Example: Before choosing a college, he gathered information from multiple sources to ensure he made an informed choice

* * *

ACTIVITY 1:

Fill out the blanks with the appropriate idioms in italics given below.

Isabel was _____1_____when she decided to throw a surprise party for her boss. She had always been _____2_____trying to get a promotion, but this event made her _____3_____. She knew she _____4_____that was amazing, or she would _____5_____.

The day of the party arrived, and Isabel _____6_____making sure everything was perfect. Just when she thought she could finally relax, the cake arrived and it was _____7_____that it was the wrong flavor. "Great," she muttered to herself, "Now I really am _____8_____.

Despite the hiccups, the party went off without a hitch. Her boss was thrilled, and Isabel could tell by the end of the night that she was _____9_____. It seemed her hard work had finally paid off.

* * *

in over her head

in a tight spot

feel ill at ease.

had to impress her boss with a party

incriminate herself.

was in the driver's seat,

immediately obvious

in a jam.

in her boss' good books.

A RECAP OF IDIOMS LEARNT: CAN YOU GUESS THE MEANING OF THESE SENTENCES?

- Without a job, she had too much free time and, as they say, idle minds are the devil's workshop. She started pushing drugs, and her ill-gotten gains eventually got her into hot water.

- She jumped into the project with both feet, but soon realized she was in over her head.

If you feel you are in need of more help, do read about one-to-one coaching in the Afterword (at the end of this book)

IDIOMS BEGINNING WITH J

*H*ere's the 100:

1 JACK OF ALL TRADES

Meaning: A person who can do many different types of work.

Example: He's a jack of all trades and can fix almost anything.

Example: As a jack of all trades, she handled the entire project herself.

2 JACK UP

Meaning: To raise or increase suddenly.

Example: They decided to jack up the prices due to high demand.

Example: The company jacked up the prices of their products last month.

3 JACK UP THE PRICE

Meaning: To increase the price significantly.

Example: They jacked up the price of tickets for the concert.

Example: The store jacked up the price of water during the heatwave.

4 JACK-OF-ALL-TRADES, MASTER OF NONE

Meaning: Someone who can do many things but is not an expert in any of them.

Example: He's a jack-of-all-trades, master of none.

Example: While being versatile is good, don't be a jack-of-all-trades master of none.

5 JAB SOMETHING INTO SOMETHING

Meaning: To push or thrust something sharply into something else.

Example: He jabbed the needle into the fabric.

Example: She jabbed the pen into the paper, making a hole.

6 JABBED A FINGER

Meaning: To point or poke sharply with a finger.

Example: He jabbed a finger at the map to show the location.

Example: She jabbed a finger in his direction to emphasize her point.

7 JAGGED EDGE

Meaning: An edge that is uneven or sharp, often dangerous.

Example: The broken glass had a jagged edge that could easily cut someone.

Example: Be careful of the jagged edge on that piece of metal.

8 JAM ON THE BRAKES

Meaning: To suddenly apply the brakes of a vehicle.

Example: He had to jam on the brakes to avoid hitting the dog.

Example: She jammed on the brakes when the car in front stopped suddenly.

9 JAM-PACKED

Meaning: Completely full or crowded.

Example: The stadium was jam-packed with fans.

Example: Her schedule is jam-packed with meetings.

10 JAM UP

Meaning: To block or obstruct something.

Example: The printer jammed up and stopped working.

Example: Traffic jammed up on the highway due to an accident.

11 JANE DOE

Meaning: A name used for an unidentified female.

Example: The hospital admitted a Jane Doe last night.

Example: The court case listed her as Jane Doe to protect her rights.

12 JAR ON MY NERVES

Meaning: To irritate or annoy someone.

Example: The constant noise from the construction site was jarring on my nerves.

Example: His habit of tapping his pen jars on my nerves.

13 JAW DROPPING

Meaning: Describes something so surprising, impressive, or shocking that it causes someone's jaw to drop open in amazement.

Example: The special effects in the movie were jaw-dropping; I've never seen anything like it.

Example: The scenic view from the top of the mountain was absolutely jaw-dropping.

14 JAWS OF DEATH/DEFEAT

Meaning: A situation where someone narrowly escapes a dangerous or disastrous outcome.

Example: The firefighters saved the family from the jaws of death.

Example: The team managed to snatch victory from the jaws of defeat.

15 JAUNDICED EYE

Meaning: A biased or cynical view.

Example: He looked at the proposal with a jaundiced eye, doubting its success.

Example: Given his past behavior, she viewed his promises with a jaundiced eye.

16 JAUNDICED VIEW

Meaning: A cynical or negative outlook.

Example: After years in politics, he had developed a jaundiced view of human nature.

Example: Her jaundiced view of the industry made her skeptical of any new trends.

17 JEALOUSLY GUARDED

Meaning: Protected or kept with great care to avoid loss or damage.

Example: The chef jealously guards the recipe for the famous sauce.

Example: She jealously guarded her privacy from the media.

18 JET LAG

Meaning: The feeling of tiredness and confusion after a long flight across different time zones.

Example: She experienced severe jet lag after her flight from New York to Tokyo.

Example: It took him a few days to recover from the jet lag after traveling to Europe.

19 JET SET

Meaning: A wealthy and fashionable group of people who travel frequently.

Example: She lives a jet-set lifestyle, always traveling to exotic places.

Example: The jet set gathered in Monaco for the annual event.

20 JERK OF HIS HEAD

Meaning: A sudden, quick movement of the head, often used to signal or indicate something.

Example: He gave a quick jerk of his head to signal that it was time to leave.

Example: With a jerk of his head, he indicated the direction they should go.

21 JEWEL IN THE CROWN

Meaning: The most valuable or prized part of something.

Example: The new software is the jewel in the crown of their product line.

Example: The city's historic district is considered the jewel in the crown of its tourism industry.

22 JOB DONE

Meaning: A phrase used to indicate that a task has been completed successfully.

Example: After fixing the leak, he stood up and said, "Job done."

Example: With the final report submitted, it was another job done for the team.

23 JOB OF DOING SOMETHING

Meaning: refers to the responsibility, task, or effort to complete a particular action or activity.

Example: She took on the job of organizing the entire event from start to finish.

Example: The manager gave him the job of handling all customer complaints for the week.

24 JOB SATISFACTION

Meaning: The contentment or pleasure derived from one's work.

Example: She finds excellent job satisfaction in helping her clients.

Example: High job satisfaction is often linked to better performance and productivity.

25 JOB SECURITY

Meaning: The likelihood that someone will keep their job without the risk of becoming unemployed.

Example: He values job security over a high salary.

Example: Many employees are worried about their job security with the recent layoffs.

26 JOCKEY FOR POSITION

Meaning: To try to get into a better position or situation.

Example: The competitors were jockeying for position at the start of the race.

Example: Employees often jockey for position when a promotion is available.

27 JOG SOMEONE'S MEMORY

Meaning: To help someone remember something.

Example: Seeing the old photos jogged her memory.

Example: Can you jog my memory about our meeting last week?

28 JOHNNY-COME-LATELY

Meaning: A newcomer or late arrival.

Example: He's just a Johnny-come-lately in the business world.

Example: The new employee is a Johnny-come-lately but is catching up quickly.

29 JOIN FORCES

Meaning: To work together with someone.

Example: They decided to join forces to tackle the project.

Example: The two companies joined forces to create a new product.

30 JOIN HANDS

Meaning: To work together or unite in a common cause.

Example: The community decided to join hands to clean up the park.

Example: Let's join hands to make this project a success.

31 JOIN THE CLUB

Meaning: To share a similar experience or problem as someone else.

Example: You're tired? Join the club.

Example: He said, "Join the club," when I told him I was feeling overwhelmed.

32 JOIN THE FRAY

Meaning: To become involved in an argument or fight.

Example: He decided to join the fray and defend his position.

Example: She joined the fray to support her friend.

33 JOIN THE RANKS

Meaning: To become part of a group.

Example: She joined the ranks of successful entrepreneurs.

Example: After graduation, he joined the ranks of the unemployed.

34 JOINED AT THE HIP

Meaning: Very closely connected or inseparable.

Example: Those two friends are joined at the hip; they do everything together.

Example: Since they started the business, they've been joined at the hip.

35 JOINT EFFORT

Meaning: A collaborative effort by two or more people or groups.

Example: The project was a joint effort between the marketing and sales teams.

Example: Cleaning up the beach was a joint effort by the local community.

36 JOINT VENTURE

Meaning: A business or project undertaken by two or more parties, typically sharing risks and rewards.

Example: The companies formed a joint venture to develop new technology.

Example: Our joint venture with the local firm has been very successful.

37 JOKING APART

Meaning: Used to indicate that what follows is serious after making a joke.

Example: Joking apart, we really need to focus on this project if we want to meet the deadline.

Example: Joking apart, you should get that injury checked by a doctor.

38 JOLLY GOOD

Meaning: Excellent or very good (often used in British English).

Example: You did a jolly good job on the presentation!

Example: It was a jolly good idea to go on a picnic.

39 JOLLY WELL

Meaning: Emphatically, used to stress the importance or certainty of something (often used in British English).

Example: You should jolly well finish your homework before you go out.

Example: He jolly well knew what he was doing was wrong.

40 JOLT SOMEBODY/SOMETHING INTO

Meaning: To shock or surprise someone or something into taking action or to abruptly prompt a change in behavior or thinking.

Example: The alarming news jolted her into reassessing her priorities

Example: The economic crisis jolted the government into implementing new policies.

41 JOT DOWN

Meaning: To write something quickly.

Example: Let me jot down your phone number.

Example: She jotted down the address before she forgot.

42 JUDGE A BOOK BY ITS COVER

Meaning: To form an opinion about someone or something based solely on appearance without considering deeper qualities or characteristics.

Example: Don't judge a book by its cover; she may seem quiet, but she's very talented.

Example: He learned not to judge a book by its cover after discovering how interesting the seemingly dull book was.

43 JUDGE THE SUCCESS OF SOMETHING

Meaning: To evaluate or determine how well something has achieved its goals.

Example: You can't judge the success of a project until all the results are in.

Example: We will judge the success of the new marketing campaign by the increase in sales.

44 JUDGING BY/FROM SOMETHING

Meaning: To form an opinion or deduce based on specific evidence or observations.

Example: Judging by his tone, he wasn't pleased with the decision.

Example: Judging from the dark clouds, it looks like it will rain soon.

45 JUDGMENT CALL

Meaning: A decision made based on one's personal judgment or discretion, especially when there is no clear right or wrong answer.

Example: Deciding whether to cancel the outdoor event due to weather was a tough judgment call.

Example: The referee's judgment call on the penalty sparked much debate among the fans.

46 JUGGLING ACT

Meaning: refers to the challenge of managing multiple tasks, responsibilities, or demands at the same time.

Example: Being a single parent with a full-time job feels like a constant juggling act

Example: Running a business while studying for exams turned into a juggling act for her.

47 JUGGLE TOO MANY BALLS

Meaning: To try to handle many tasks at the same time.

Example: She's juggling too many balls with work, school, and family.

Example: He feels like he's juggling too many balls and can't keep up.

48 JUICY GOSSIP/DETAILS

Meaning: Interesting and often scandalous information or stories.

Example: She couldn't wait to share the juicy gossip she had heard about their coworker.

Example: The magazine article was full of juicy details about the celebrity's private life.

49 JUMP A LIGHT

Meaning: Go through a traffic light when it is red or about to change to red.

Example: He was fined for jumping a red light at the intersection.

Example: It's dangerous to jump a light, especially during rush hour.

50 JUMP AT SHADOWS

Meaning: To be very nervous and easily frightened.

Example: After the robbery, she was jumping at shadows.

Example: He's been jumping at shadows since the accident.

51 JUMP AT THE CHANCE

Meaning: To eagerly accept an opportunity.

Example: When he offered her the job, she jumped at the chance.

Example: I'd jump at the chance to travel to Europe.

52 JUMP BAIL

Meaning: To fail to appear in court after being released on bail.

Example: The suspect jumped bail and is now a fugitive.

Example: They were worried he might jump bail and disappear.

53 JUMP CLEAR OF SOMETHING

Meaning: To quickly move away or leap out of the way to avoid danger, harm, or an impact.

Example: The driver managed to jump clear of the car just before it caught fire.

Example: She had to jump clear of the falling debris during the construction accident.

54 JUMP DOWN SOMEONE'S THROAT

Meaning: To suddenly speak angrily to someone.

Example: He jumped down my throat when I suggested he was wrong.

Example: Don't jump down my throat; I was just asking a question.

55 JUMP FOR JOY

Meaning: To be extremely happy or excited about something.

Example: She jumped for joy when she heard the good news.

Example: The kids jumped for joy when they saw the surprise.

56 JUMP IN FEET FIRST

Meaning: To get involved in something quickly and completely.

Example: He jumped in feet first and took on the new project.

Example: They jumped in feet first without fully understanding the risks.

57 JUMP OFF THE DEEP END

Meaning: To act recklessly or suddenly without thinking.

Example: He jumped off the deep end and quit his job without any backup plan.

Example: She jumped off the deep end and invested all her money in one stock.

58 JUMP ON THE BANDWAGON

Meaning: To join others in doing something that is currently popular.

Example: Many companies are jumping on the bandwagon of social media marketing.

Example: He decided to jump on the bandwagon and start using the new app.

59 JUMP OUT AT

Meaning: To be very noticeable or striking; to immediately attract attention.

Example: The bright colors of the painting really jump out at you.

Example: Her name jumped out at me from the list of participants.

60 JUMP OUT OF ONE'S SKIN

Meaning: To be very startled or surprised.

Example: She nearly jumped out of her skin when the phone rang.

Example: He jumped out of his skin at the loud noise.

61 JUMP OUT OF THE FRYING PAN INTO THE FIRE

Meaning: To go from a bad situation to a worse one.

Example: He left his low-paying job for a high-stress one. He jumped out of the frying pan into the fire.

Example: Moving to a new city without a job was like jumping out of the frying pan into the fire.

62 JUMP SHIP

Meaning: To leave a job or activity suddenly.

Example: He jumped ship to join a rival company.

Example: Several employees jumped ship after the company was sold.

63 JUMP THE GUN

Meaning: To start something too early or prematurely.

Example: She jumped the gun and announced their engagement before he proposed.

Example: They jumped the gun by launching the product without proper testing.

64 JUMP THE QUEUE

Meaning: To cut in line ahead of others.

Example: It's not fair to jump the queue.

Example: He was caught trying to jump the queue at the concert.

65 JUMP THROUGH HOOPS

Meaning: To go through many complex tasks to achieve something.

Example: He had to jump through hoops to get his visa approved.

Example: They made us jump through hoops to get the project approved.

Jump through hoops

66 JUMP TO CONCLUSIONS

Meaning: To make a hasty judgment without knowing all the facts.

Example: Don't jump to conclusions; let's gather all the information first.

Example: She jumped to conclusions and blamed him for the mistake.

67 JUMP TO IT

Meaning: To start doing something quickly.

Example: We need to jump to it to finish on time.

Example: He told them to jump to it and finish the work.

68 JUMP TO ONE'S FEET

Meaning: To stand up quickly.

Example: He jumped to his feet when he heard the news.

Example: She jumped to her feet to greet the visitors.

69 JUMP TO THE CONCLUSION

Meaning: To decide something quickly without having all the facts.

Example: He jumped to the conclusion that she was lying.

Example: Don't jump to the conclusion until you have all the details.

70 JUMPING JACK

Meaning: A physical exercise where one jumps to a position with the legs spread wide and the hands touching overhead, then returns to a position with the feet together and the arms at the sides.

Example: We started our workout with a series of jumping jacks.

Example: The coach instructed the players to do 20 jumping jacks as a warm-up.

71 JUST A DROP IN THE BUCKET

Meaning: A very small part of something much bigger.

Example: His donation was just a drop in the bucket compared to what was needed.

Example: One person's efforts to save the environment may seem like just a drop in the bucket.

72 JUST A MINUTE/SECOND/MOMENT

Meaning: A request for someone to wait briefly or a short period of time.

Example: Just a second, I'll be right with you.

Example: Just a moment, let me finish this call.

73 JUST A MOMENT

Meaning: A short period of time.

Example: I'll be with you in just a moment.

Example: Just a moment, let me finish this task.

74 JUST A STONE'S THROW AWAY

Meaning: Very close in distance.

Example: The park is just a stone's throw away from my house.

Example: Her office is just a stone's throw away from the train station.

75 JUST ABOUT

Meaning: Almost; nearly.

Example: I'm just about ready to leave.

Example: The project is just about finished.

76 JUST AROUND THE CORNER

Meaning: Something is about to happen soon.

Example: With graduation just around the corner, she started applying for jobs.

Example: The holidays are just around the corner.

77 JUST AS GOOD/BAD AS

Meaning: Used to compare two things or situations as being equally good or bad.

Example: The movie was just as good as I expected it to be.

Example: Missing the deadline is just as bad as not completing the task at all.

78 JUST AS SOON

Meaning: Equally prefer or be willing to do one thing as another.

Example: I'd just as soon stay home as go out tonight.

Example: He said he'd just as soon take the bus as drive.

79 JUST BECAUSE...IT DOESN'T MEAN THAT

Meaning: Used to point out that one fact does not necessarily lead to or prove another.

Example: Just because he's quiet, it doesn't mean he's not paying attention.

Example: Just because it's expensive, it doesn't mean it's the best option.

80 JUST BETWEEN YOU AND ME

Meaning: In confidence; privately.

Example: Just between you and me, I think he's making a big mistake.

Example: Just between you and me, she's planning to leave the company.

81 JUST DESERTS

Meaning: The punishment that one deserves.

Example: He finally got his just deserts for cheating.

Example: The villain received his just deserts in the end.

82 JUST FOR KICKS

Meaning: For fun or amusement.

Example: They went skydiving just for kicks.

Example: She dyed her hair pink just for kicks.

83 JUST FOR THE RECORD

Meaning: To make something clear for future reference.

Example: Just for the record, I never agreed to that plan.

Example: Just for the record, she did apologize later.

84 JUST HAVE TO DO SOMETHING

Meaning: Used to express that there is no alternative but to do something or that it is necessary.

Example: If the deadline is tomorrow, we'll just have to work late.

Example: If you want the job, you'll just have to keep applying.

85 JUST IN CASE

Meaning: As a precaution.

Example: Take an umbrella, just in case it rains.

Example: She brought extra snacks, just in case they got hungry.

86 JUST IN THE NICK OF TIME

Meaning: At the last possible moment.

Example: They made it to the station just in the nick of time.

Example: The firefighters arrived just in the nick of time.

87 JUST MY LUCK

Meaning: Used to express frustration or disappointment at one's own bad luck.

Example: The bus left just as I arrived. Just my luck!

Example: It started raining right after I washed my car—just my luck.

88. JUST NOW

Meaning: Refers to something that happened very recently or a moment ago.

Example: She left just now; you might still catch her.

Example: I was looking for my keys just now, and now they're gone again.

89 JUST OFF THE BOAT

Meaning: Naive or inexperienced.

Example: He's just off the boat and doesn't understand how things work here.

Example: She seems just off the boat regarding city life.

90 JUST PASSING THROUGH

Meaning: To be in a place temporarily.

Example: I'm just passing through town on my way to the coast.

Example: She was just passing through and decided to visit an old friend.

91 JUST THE CLOTHES ON HIS BACK

Meaning: Having nothing other than the clothes one wears usually implies that someone has lost everything or is starting over with very little.

Example: After the fire destroyed their home, the family was left with just the clothes on their backs, but they were grateful to be safe.

Example: When John moved to a new city to start fresh, he arrived with just the clothes on his back and a determination to build a better life.

92 JUST THE SAME

Meaning: Despite differences or circumstances, similarly or nonetheless.

Example: I told him not to go out in the storm, but he went just the same.

Example: She wasn't feeling well but showed up just the same.

93 JUST THE TICKET

Meaning: Exactly what is needed.

Example: A relaxing day at the spa was just the ticket.

Example: This book is just the ticket for a rainy afternoon.

94 JUST THINK/IMAGINE

Meaning: Used to encourage someone to consider or picture a particular situation or outcome, often surprising or exciting.

Example: Just imagine living in a house by the sea with that view every day.

Example: Just think how amazing it would be to travel the world.

95 JUST WHAT THE DOCTOR ORDERED

Meaning: Exactly what is needed or wanted.

Example: A vacation in the sun is just what the doctor ordered.

Example: The hot soup was just what the doctor ordered on a cold day.

96 JUSTIFY DOING SOMETHING

Meaning: To provide valid reasons or explanations for an action.

Example: How can you justify spending so much money on clothes?

Example: He tried to justify taking the day off by saying he felt unwell.

97 JUSTIFY YOURSELF

Meaning: To explain or defend your actions or decisions.

Example: She needed to justify herself when questioned about her choices.

Example: He didn't feel he had to justify himself to anyone.

98 JUSTIFICATION FOR DOING SOMETHING

Meaning: A reason or explanation for taking a specific action.

Example: The company provided a justification for laying off workers.

Example: What's your justification for leaving the meeting early?

99 JUSTIFIED IN DOING SOMETHING

Meaning: Having a valid reason or being right in taking a particular action.

Example: She felt justified in her decision to quit the job due to the poor working conditions.

Example: He was justified in calling the police after witnessing the crime.

100 JUSTICE HAS BEEN DONE

Meaning: A fair or just outcome has been achieved.

Example: After the trial, the victims' families felt that justice had been done.

Example: The judge's decision ensured that justice had been done.

* * *

ACTIVITY 2

Fill in the blanks with the idioms given below in italics.

Jordan had always yearned for a life of adventure, so even though he did not have much money, he decided to _____1_____ and travel the world. But the journey _____2_____. He quickly realized that life on the road wasn't as glamorous as he had imagined. He often found himself in _____3_____ buses, traveling for hours on end with _____4_____.

During one particularly rough day, Jordan felt like _____5_____. The rain was pouring, his phone was dead, and he was lost in a foreign city. But then, out of nowhere, a local offered him shelter and a hot meal. "Sometimes," Jordan thought, "you just have to _____6_____ when life offers you a bit of kindness."

By the end of his journey, Jordan understood that while his trip was filled with challenges, those hardships had made the experience all the more rewarding. It wasn't always easy, but he was glad he didn't _____7_____ about quitting early.

* * *

jump off the deep end

jarred on his nerves

jam-packed

just the clothes on his back.

jumping ship

jump at the chance

jump to the conclusion

A RECAP OF IDIOMS LEARNT: CAN YOU GUESS THE MEANING OF THESE SENTENCES?

- He was trying to juggle too many tasks at once and ended up jumping the gun on an important decision.
- She decided to jump on the bandwagon when she saw how successful the new trend was.

If you need more help, there is one-to-one coaching in the After-word section at the end of the book.

IDIOMS BEGINNING WITH K

*H*ere's the 100:

1 KEEP A LOW PROFILE

Meaning: To avoid attracting attention.

Example: After the scandal, he decided to keep a low profile.

Example: She kept a low profile during the investigation.

2 KEEP A STIFF UPPER LIP

Meaning: To be brave and not show emotion in a difficult situation.

Example: Even during the crisis, he kept a stiff upper lip.

Example: She kept a stiff upper lip throughout the entire ordeal.

3 KEEP AN EAR TO THE GROUND

Meaning: To stay informed about current events or trends.

Example: It's important to keep an ear to the ground in the tech industry.

Example: She keeps an ear to the ground to hear about any new job opportunities.

Keep an ear to the ground

4 KEEP AN EYE ON

Meaning: To watch or look after something or someone.

Example: Can you keep an eye on my bag while I go to the restroom?

Example: They kept an eye on the weather forecast for their outdoor event.

5 KEEP AT BAY

Meaning: To prevent something from approaching or having an effect.

Example: She used insect repellent to keep the mosquitoes at bay.

Example: The medication helped keep the pain at bay.

6 KEEP BODY AND SOUL TOGETHER

Meaning: To survive, especially with difficulty.

Example: Despite the hard times, she managed to keep body and soul together.

Example: He worked two jobs to keep body and soul together.

7 KEEP GOING

Meaning: To continue persevering or proceeding, especially in the face of difficulties.

Example: Even though the climb was tough, she told herself to keep going until she reached the top.

Example: He faced many setbacks but decided to keep going with his business plans.

8 KEEP IN MIND

Meaning: To remember or consider something.

Example: Keep in mind that the store closes early on Sundays.

Example: She kept in mind the advice her mentor gave her.

9 KEEP IT UNDER WRAPS

Meaning: To keep something secret.

Example: They kept the surprise party under wraps until the last minute.

Example: The company kept the new product development under wraps.

10 KEEP ONE'S CHIN UP

Meaning: To remain cheerful and hopeful during difficult times.

Example: Despite the setbacks, she kept her chin up.

Example: He told his friend to keep his chin up after losing the job.

11 KEEP ONE'S COOL

Meaning: To remain calm and composed.

Example: She managed to keep her cool during the argument.

Example: He kept his cool even when the situation became tense.

12 KEEP ONE'S DISTANCE

Meaning: To maintain a safe or respectful distance from someone or something.

Example: He kept his distance from the argument.

Example: They kept their distance from the wild animal.

13 KEEP ONE'S EYE ON THE BALL

Meaning: To stay focused on the main goal or objective.

Example: If you want to succeed, keep your eye on the ball.

Example: She kept her eye on the ball and achieved her targets.

14 KEEP ONE'S FINGERS CROSSED

Meaning: To hope for a positive outcome.

Example: I'm keeping my fingers crossed for good weather tomorrow.

Example: She kept her fingers crossed while waiting for the exam results.

15 KEEP ONE'S HEAD ABOVE WATER

Meaning: To manage to survive or maintain a situation despite difficulties.

Example: With all the bills to pay, he's barely keeping his head above water.

Example: They struggled to keep their heads above water during the economic downturn.

16 KEEP ONE'S HEAD DOWN

Meaning: To avoid attracting attention or getting involved in trouble.

Example: During the meeting, he kept his head down and didn't say much.

Example: She kept her head down and focused on her work.

17 KEEP ONE'S NOSE CLEAN

Meaning: To avoid trouble or wrongdoing.

Example: He kept his nose clean and stayed out of trouble after his release.

Example: She advised her son to keep his nose clean while at college.

18 KEEP ONE'S OPTIONS OPEN

Meaning: To avoid making a decision now so that one still has a choice in the future.

Example: She's keeping her options open regarding her career path.

Example: They decided to keep their options open before committing to a new house.

19 KEEP PACE WITH

Meaning: To stay level or equal with someone or something.

Example: It's hard to keep pace with the fast technological changes.

Example: She struggled to keep pace with her more experienced colleagues.

20 KEEP SOMEBODY AT SOMETHING

Meaning: To encourage or force someone to continue doing something.

Example: The coach kept the team at their drills until they perfected their technique.

Example: She kept him at his studies until he finished his homework.

21 KEEP SOMEBODY UP

Meaning: To prevent someone from going to bed or sleeping.

Example: The noise from the party kept her up all night.

Example: He was kept up late by his work deadlines.

22 KEEP SOMETHING QUIET

Meaning: To keep something secret or undisclosed.

Example: They decided to keep the promotion quiet until all the employees were notified.

Example: She kept the news about her new job quiet until everything was finalized.

23 KEEP SOMETHING TO YOURSELF

Meaning: To not share information or feelings with others; to keep something private.

Example: He decided to keep his doubts to himself rather than worry his friends.

Example: She kept her plans to herself until she was sure they would work out.

24 KEEP TABS ON

Meaning: To monitor or watch closely.

Example: They kept tabs on the competitor's activities.

Example: She kept tabs on her spending to avoid going over budget.

25 KEEP THE BALL ROLLING

Meaning: To maintain progress or momentum.

Example: Let's keep the ball rolling with this project.

Example: They kept the ball rolling with their fundraising efforts.

26 KEEP THE FAITH

Meaning: To remain optimistic or hopeful, especially in difficult times.

Example: Despite the challenges, he kept the faith that things would improve.

Example: She encouraged her team to keep the faith during the crisis.

27 KEEP THE PEACE

Meaning: To maintain or restore order and prevent conflict.

Example: The police were there to keep the peace during the protest.

Example: She played a key role in keeping the peace at family gatherings.

28 KEEP THE WOLF FROM THE DOOR

Meaning: To have just enough money to avoid hunger or poverty.

Example: He took on extra work to keep the wolf from the door.

Example: They managed to keep the wolf from the door despite their financial struggles.

29 KEEP TO ONESELF

Meaning: To avoid social interaction and not share personal information.

Example: He tends to keep to himself and doesn't socialize much.

Example: She kept to herself after moving to the new neighborhood.

30 KEEP UNDER CONTROL

Meaning: To manage or restrain something effectively.

Example: They managed to keep the fire under control.

Example: She kept her emotions under control during the meeting.

31 KEEP UP APPEARANCES

Meaning: To maintain an outward show of prosperity or well-being despite difficulties.

Example: They struggled to keep up appearances after losing their jobs.

Example: She kept up appearances even though she was feeling stressed.

32 KEEP UP THE GOOD WORK

Meaning: To continue doing something well.

Example: Your progress is impressive. Keep up the good work!

Example: The manager encouraged his team to keep up the good work.

33 KEEP UP WITH

Meaning: To stay informed or remain at the same level as someone or something.

Example: It's hard to keep up with the latest trends in fashion.

Example: He struggled to keep up with his classmates in math.

34 KEEP YOUR NOSE TO THE GRINDSTONE

Meaning: To work hard and consistently.

Example: If you keep your nose to the grindstone, you'll finish the project on time.

Example: She kept her nose to the grindstone to achieve her career goals.

35 KEEP YOURSELF FROM DOING SOMETHING

Meaning: To prevent yourself from doing something.

Example: He couldn't keep himself from laughing during the serious moment.

Example: She had to keep herself from eating all the cookies in one sitting.

36 KEEP YOURSELF TO YOURSELF

Meaning: To avoid socializing or sharing personal information with others.

Example: He prefers to keep himself to himself and doesn't attend many social events.

Example: Since moving to the new neighborhood, she's been keeping herself to herself.

37 KEEP YOUR SPIRITS/MORALE/STRENGTH UP

Meaning: To stay positive, motivated, or strong during difficult times.

Example: Despite the setbacks, she kept her spirits up.

Example: He encouraged the team to keep their morale up throughout the tough project.

38 KEEN FOR SOMETHING TO HAPPEN

Meaning: Eager or enthusiastic for a particular event or situation to occur.

Example: They are keen for the new policy to be implemented.

Example: She is keen for the meeting to start on time.

39 KEEN ON DOING SOMETHING

Meaning: Very interested or enthusiastic about doing something.

Example: She is keen on learning new languages.

Example: He's keen on joining the basketball team.

40 KEY FACTOR/POINTS/QUESTION

Meaning: The most important element or aspect of a situation or discussion.

Example: The key factor in their success was effective teamwork.

Example: During the meeting, they discussed the key points of the proposal.

Example: The key question is how to increase productivity without increasing costs.

41 KEYNOTE/SPEECH/ADDRESS/LECTURE

Meaning: The main or most important speech at a gathering or event.

Example: The CEO delivered the keynote address at the conference.

Example: Her keynote speech inspired everyone at the event.

42 KICK A HABIT

Meaning: To stop doing something harmful that one has done for a long time.

Example: He finally managed to kick his smoking habit.

Example: She struggled to kick the habit of biting her nails.

43 KICK AROUND

Meaning: To discuss or consider an idea or plan.

Example: Let's kick around some ideas for the new project.

Example: They kicked around several options before making a decision.

44 KICK BACK

Meaning: To relax and take it easy.

Example: After a long day at work, he likes to kick back and watch TV.

Example: They kicked back on the beach during their vacation.

45 KICK IN

Meaning: To start to take effect.

Example: The painkillers began to kick in after about 20 minutes.

Example: The new regulations will kick in next month.

46 KICK OFF

Meaning: To start or begin something.

Example: The conference will kick off with a keynote speech.

Example: They kicked off the meeting with a round of introductions.

47 KICK ONESELF

Meaning: To regret something one did or did not do.

Example: He kicked himself for not buying the stock when it was cheap.

Example: She was kicking herself for missing the opportunity.

48 KICK OUT

Meaning: To force someone to leave a place or position.

Example: He was kicked out of the bar for causing trouble.

Example: They decided to kick out the member who was not cooperative.

49 KICK SOMEBODY IN THE TEETH

Meaning: To treat someone very badly or disappoint them when they are already in a difficult situation.

Example: Losing his job was a real kick in the teeth, especially right before the holidays.

Example: After all his hard work, the unfair criticism felt like a kick in the teeth.

50 KICK SOMEBODY WHEN THEY ARE DOWN

Meaning: To make someone's difficult situation even worse by criticizing or hurting them when they are already vulnerable.

Example: Criticizing him after he lost his job was like kicking him when he was down.

Example: It's unfair to kick someone when they are down; they need support, not more problems.

51 KICK THE BUCKET

Meaning: To die.

Example: He was devastated when his pet turtle kicked the bucket.

Example: The old man joked about not being ready to kick the bucket yet.

Kick the bucket

52 KICK THE HABIT

Meaning: To stop doing something that is a habit, especially something harmful.

Example: She tried to kick the habit of eating junk food.

Example: He finally managed to kick the habit of procrastinating.

53 KICK UP A FUSS

Meaning: To complain or create a disturbance about something.

Example: The customers kicked up a fuss about the poor service.

Example: She kicked up a fuss when her flight was delayed.

54 KICK UP ONE'S HEELS

Meaning: To enjoy oneself and have a good time.

Example: They kicked up their heels at the wedding reception.

Example: After the exams, the students kicked up their heels and celebrated.

55 KICK YOUR HEELS

Meaning: To waste time waiting for something to happen.

Example: We had to kick our heels for an hour before the meeting started.

Example: He was kicking his heels in the waiting room, bored out of his mind.

56 KICKED INTO GEAR

Meaning: To start working effectively or efficiently.

Example: The team kicked into gear as the deadline approached.

Example: The new marketing strategy kicked into gear this month.

57 KICKING AND SCREAMING

Meaning: To do something reluctantly and with strong resistance.

Example: He went to the dentist kicking and screaming.

Example: She was dragged to the party, kicking and screaming.

58 KID GLOVES

Meaning: To treat someone or something very gently or carefully.

Example: They handled the negotiations with kid gloves to avoid upsetting anyone.

Example: The manager used kid gloves when dealing with the new employees.

59 KID YOURSELF THAT

Meaning: To convince yourself of something that is not true.

Example: Don't kid yourself that you can finish the project without help.

Example: She tried to kid herself that everything was fine, but she knew it wasn't.

60 KILL TWO BIRDS WITH ONE STONE

Meaning: To accomplish multiple tasks with a single action.

Example: By combining errands, she was able to kill two birds with one stone.

Example: The new policy aims to kill two birds with one stone by improving efficiency and reducing costs.

61 KILL SOMEBODY WITH KINDNESS

Meaning: To be excessively kind or helpful to someone, often to the point of being annoying or harmful.

Example: Her mother tried to kill her with kindness by doing everything for her.

Example: They killed him with kindness, always fussing over him and not giving him any space.

62 KILL TIME

Meaning: To do something to pass the time while waiting for something else.

Example: We killed time at the airport by reading magazines.

Example: He killed time by watching TV until his friends arrived.

63 KILL THE GOOSE THAT LAYS THE GOLDEN EGG

Meaning: To ruin or destroy a source of continuous profit or benefit through greed or short-sighted actions.

Example: By overworking the top salesperson without any reward, the company killed the goose that laid the golden egg when she left for a competitor.

Example: The local government raised taxes on tourism so high that it killed the goose that lays the golden egg, as visitors stopped coming to the area.

64 KILLING IT

Meaning: To do something extremely well.

Example: She's killing it at her new job.

Example: The band is really killing it on their tour.

65 KINDRED SPIRIT

Meaning: A person who shares similar interests, values, or feelings.

Example: They quickly became friends, recognizing each other as kindred spirits.

Example: She found a kindred spirit in her new coworker.

66 KISS AND MAKE UP

Meaning: To reconcile and become friends again after an argument.

Example: After their fight, they decided to kiss and make up.

Example: It's time to kiss and make up after all these years of estrangement.

67 KISS SOMETHING BETTER

Meaning: To make something better, often used by parents to comfort children with minor injuries.

Example: She kissed it better when her son fell and hurt his knee.

Example: He kissed her hand better after she burned it on the stove.

68 KISS SOMETHING GOODBYE

Meaning: To accept that you have lost something or will not be able to have it.

Example: After the mistake, he had to kiss goodbye to his promotion.

Example: She kissed goodbye to her vacation plans when the project deadline was moved up.

69 KNEE-DEEP IN

Meaning: Involved in something to a great extent.

Example: He's knee-deep in paperwork right now.

Example: She was knee-deep in planning the event.

70 KNEE-JERK REACTION

Meaning: An immediate and emotional response without thought.

Example: His knee-jerk reaction was to blame the new policies.

Example: She had a knee-jerk reaction to the criticism and got defensive.

71 KNACK FOR DOING SOMETHING

Meaning: A natural talent or skill for doing something.

Example: She has a knack for solving complex problems.

Example: He discovered his knack for painting during a weekend class.

72 KNOCK IT OFF

Meaning: To stop doing something annoying or disruptive.

Example: The teacher told the students to knock it off.

Example: He was being loud, so I told him to knock it off.

73 KNOCK OFF

Meaning: To stop working or doing something, often for a break or at the end of the day.

Example: Let's knock off early and grab a drink.

Example: We usually knock off work at 5 p.m.

92 KNOCK ON DOORS

Meaning: To go from place to place, usually seeking support, assistance, or opportunities.

Example: He spent months knocking on doors, trying to find a job.

Example: The politician knocked on doors in the neighborhood to gain support for her campaign.

75 KNOCK ON WOOD

Meaning: A phrase used to avoid bad luck after making a favorable statement.

Example: I've never had an accident, knock on wood.

Example: Knock on wood, we haven't had any issues so far.

76 KNOCK ONE'S SOCKS OFF

Meaning: To amaze or impress someone greatly.

Example: The performance really knocked my socks off.

Example: The new product is going to knock everyone's socks off.

77 KNOCK OUT OF THE PARK

Meaning: To do something exceptionally well.

Example: She knocked her presentation out of the park.

Example: The team knocked it out of the park with their latest project.

78 KNOCK SOME SENSE INTO SOMEBODY

Meaning: To make someone understand or behave more sensibly, often through stern or forceful means.

Example: I need to knock some sense into him; he's been making poor decisions lately.

Example: Her friends tried to knock some sense into her about her reckless behavior.

79 KNOCK SOMEBODY DOWN TO SOMETHING

Meaning: To persuade someone to reduce the price or amount of something.

Example: I managed to knock the seller down to $50 for the antique vase.

Example: She knocked him down to a lower price for the car.

80 KNOCK SOMEBODY OFF THEIR PEDESTAL/PERCH

Meaning: To bring someone down from a position of high status or arrogance.

Example: The scandal knocked the politician off his pedestal.

Example: Her unexpected defeat knocked her off her perch as the reigning champion.

81 KICK SOMEBODY'S HEAD/FACE/TEETH IN

Meaning: To beat someone severely (often used figuratively).

Example: I'll kick your teeth in if you don't stop bothering me.

Example: The bully threatened to kick his head in if he didn't hand over his lunch money.

82 KNOCK SOMEBODY'S HEADS TOGETHER

Meaning: To scold or forcefully make people cooperate or behave better.

Example: If those kids don't stop fighting, I will knock their heads together.

Example: The manager had to knock their heads together to get them to work as a team.

83 KNOCK SOMETHING DOWN

Meaning: To demolish or destroy a building or structure.

Example: They plan to knock the old warehouse down and build a new shopping center.

Example: The storm knocked several trees down in the neighborhood.

84 KNOCK THE WIND OUT OF SOMEONE'S SAILS

Meaning: To discourage or deflate someone's enthusiasm.

Example: The bad news really knocked the wind out of his sails.

Example: Her criticism knocked the wind out of his sails.

85 KNOW BETTER

Meaning: To have the wisdom or experience to avoid making mistakes or know the right thing to do.

Example: You should know better than to leave your keys in the car.

Example: She knew better than to argue with her boss in front of the team.

86 KNOW DIFFERENT/OTHERWISE

Meaning: To be aware that the reality or truth of a situation is different from what has been stated or assumed.

Example: He said he was going to the library, but I know different; he went to the movies instead.

Example: She claims she's fine, but I know otherwise; she's been very stressed lately.

87 KNOW IT ALL

Meaning: Someone who behaves as if they know everything.

Example: He's such a know-it-all, always correcting everyone.

Example: Her know-it-all attitude annoys her coworkers.

88 KNOW NO BOUNDS

Meaning: To be limitless; to have no restrictions or boundaries.

Example: His generosity knows no bounds; he's always helping others.

Example: Her enthusiasm for the project knows no bounds.

89 KNOW ONE'S ONIONS

Meaning: To be knowledgeable or skilled in a particular area.

Example: He really knows his onions when it comes to gardening.

Example: The chef certainly knows her onions.

90 KNOW YOUR WAY AROUND

Meaning: To be familiar with a place or system and navigate it easily.

Example: She knows her way around the city quite well.

Example: It took him a few weeks, but now he knows his way around the office.

91 KNOW SOMETHING INSIDE OUT

Meaning: To be extremely familiar with something; to know it thoroughly.

Example: She knows the software inside out and can help with any issues.

Example: He studied the textbook until he knew it inside out.

92 KNOW THE DRILL

Meaning: To be familiar with a routine or procedure.

Example: You know the drill; start by checking your email.

Example: By now, we all know the drill for the fire drill.

93 KNOW THE ROPES

Meaning: To understand the details or intricacies of a task or process.

Example: It took her a while, but she finally knows the ropes at her new job.

Example: He spent years learning the ropes of the business.

94 KNOW THE SCORE

Meaning: To be aware of a situation's essential facts or realities, especially the unpleasant or challenging ones.

Example: After years in the industry, she knows the score when it comes to handling demanding clients.

Example: He wasn't surprised by the layoff announcement—he knew the score and had already started looking for a new job.

95 KNOW WHICH WAY THE WIND IS BLOWING

Meaning: To understand the current situation or trends.

Example: Before deciding, you should know which way the wind is blowing.

Example: Politicians often know which way the wind is blowing before taking a stance.

96 KNOW YOUR OWN MIND

Meaning: To be confident and sure about what you want or believe.

Example: She knows her own mind and won't be easily swayed by others' opinions.

Example: It's important to know your own mind when making important decisions.

97 KNOW YOUR PLACE

Meaning: To be aware of your position or role in a social or hierarchical setting, often implying respect for authority or social boundaries.

Example: In her new role as an intern, she knew her place, observed the senior staff, and learned from them.

Example: He was reminded to know his place when he tried to question the board members' decisions.

98 KNOW ONE'S WAY AROUND

Meaning: To be familiar with a place or system.

Example: She knows her way around the city quite well.

Example: It took him a few weeks, but now he knows his way around the office.

99 KNUCKLE DOWN

Meaning: To start working hard.

Example: With exams approaching, it's time to knuckle down and study.

Example: He decided to knuckle down and finish the project.

100 KNUCKLE UNDER

Meaning: To give in to pressure or authority.

Example: He refused to knuckle under to their demands.

Example: She finally knuckled under and agreed to their terms.

* * *

ACTIVITY 3

Please fill in the blanks with the idioms in italics below:

Kara was known for being _____1_____ her work. She always _____2_____ for solving problems that others couldn't figure out. But when her company decided to take on a massive project, even Kara felt _____3_____daily problems, hoping everything would go smoothly.

As the deadline approached, Kara started to feel the pressure. She was _____4_____ that the new software they were developing wouldn't have any major glitches. However, a critical bug was discovered just two days before the launch. Kara knew she had to_____5_____ and find a solution quickly.

Working late into the night, she managed to _____6_____. The launch was a success, and her boss praised her for her dedication. "You really_____7_____ this time, Kara," he said with a smile. Kara couldn't help but feel proud. It wasn't easy, but she had _____8_____ and made it through.

* * *

keen on doing

knew the ropes

knee-deep in

keeping her fingers crossed

keep her cool

keep the problem under control

knocked it out of the park

kept her nose to the grindstone

A RECAP OF IDIOMS LEARNT: CAN YOU GUESS THE MEANING OF THESE SENTENCES?

- She's running out of steam, but if she keeps her eye on the ball, she'll still come out on top.

- When the rumors became unbearable for Michael Jackson, he kept a low profile; however, he felt he had to keep an ear to the ground to know when the rumors would end.

If you need more help, the Afterword section at the end of the book offers the option of one-on-one coaching with Ms A M Lucas.

IDIOMS BEGINNING WITH L

*H*ere's the 100

1 LABOR OF LOVE

Meaning: A task done for pleasure, not for reward.

Example: Her garden is a labor of love.

Example: Writing the book was a labor of love for him.

2 LAID BACK ATTITUDE

Meaning: A relaxed and easy-going demeanor.

Example: His laid back attitude helps him stay calm under pressure.

Example: She approached the project with a laid back attitude, which kept the team stress-free.

3 LAME DUCK

Meaning: An ineffectual or unsuccessful person or thing.

Example: The company became a lame duck after losing its major client.

Example: He was considered a lame duck after his injury.

4 LAND A PUNCH/BLOW

Meaning: To successfully hit someone with a punch or blow.

Example: The boxer managed to land a punch right at the start of the match.

Example: He landed a blow that knocked his opponent to the ground.

5 LAND ON ONE'S FEET

Meaning: To recover well from a setback.

Example: Despite losing his job, he landed on his feet in a new position.

Example: She always seems to land on her feet no matter what happens.

6 LAND WITH A BUMP

Meaning: To experience a sudden and often unpleasant reality check.

Example: After the vacation, returning to work made her land with a bump.

Example: He landed with a bump when he realized the project wasn't going well.

7 LARGER THAN LIFE

Meaning: More exaggerated or attractive than usual.

Example: The movie star's personality was larger than life.

Example: His adventures made him seem larger than life.

8 LAST BUT NOT LEAST

Meaning: Important, despite being mentioned last.

Example: Last but not least, we need to thank the volunteers. *Example:* The final speaker, last but not least, was the CEO.

9 LAST STRAW

Meaning: The final problem in a series that causes one to give up. *Example:* The broken air conditioner was the last straw.

Example: Her lateness was the last straw for her boss.

10 LAUGH ALL THE WAY TO THE BANK

Meaning: To make a lot of money easily.

Example: The company laughed all the way to the bank after the successful product launch.

Example: He laughed all the way to the bank after his business took off.

11 LAUGH IN SOMEONE'S FACE

Meaning: To show open disrespect or scorn.

Example: She laughed in his face when he asked for a promotion. *Example:* The proposal was so ridiculous they laughed in his face.

12 LAUGH IT OFF

Meaning: To treat something as not serious.

Example: He laughed off the criticism.

Example: She tried to laugh off the mistake.

13 LAY A FINGER ON

Meaning: To touch or harm someone.

Example: If you lay a finger on him, you'll regret it.

Example: She warned them not to lay a finger on her property.

14 LAY CLAIM TO DOING SOMETHING

Meaning: To assert that one has the right or deserves recognition for doing something, often suggesting a sense of ownership or achievement.

Example: She laid claim to developing the new strategy, highlighting her role in the project's success during the meeting.

Example: The scientist laid claim to discovering the breakthrough, ensuring her contributions were acknowledged in the research community.

15 LAY DOWN THE LAW

Meaning: To enforce rules strictly.

Example: The new manager laid down the law on the first day. *Example:* She had to lay down the law about curfews.

16 LAY EYES ON

Meaning: To see for the first time.

Example: She fell in love the moment she laid eyes on him. *Example:* He hasn't laid eyes on his hometown in years.

17 LAY IT ON THICK

Meaning: To exaggerate or overstate praise or criticism.

Example: He laid it on thick about how much he liked her cooking. *Example:* The advertisement laid it on thick about the product's benefits.

18 LAY IT ON THE LINE

Meaning: To speak frankly and directly.

Example: He laid it on the line and told her exactly what he thought.

Example: The coach laid it on the line about the team's poor performance.

19 LAY LOW

Meaning: To avoid attention or activity.

Example: After the scandal, he lay low for a while. *Example:* She laid low until the rumors died down.

20 LAY OF THE LAND

Meaning: The general state or condition of a situation.

Example: Before making a decision, he wanted to understand the lay of the land.

Example: She quickly grasped the lay of the land at her new job.

21 LAY ONE'S CARDS ON THE TABLE

Meaning: To be honest and open about one's intentions or plans. *Example:* He decided to lay his cards on the table during the negotiation.

Example: She laid her cards on the table and told him her true feelings.

22 LAY THE GROUNDWORK

Meaning: To prepare for future success.

Example: They laid the groundwork for the new project over several months.

Example: His education laid the groundwork for his successful career.

23 LEAD A CHARMED LIFE

Meaning: To be very lucky or fortunate.

Example: He seems to lead a charmed life; everything goes his way. *Example:* Despite the risks, she has always found success.

24 LEAD SOMEONE ON

Meaning: To deceive or mislead someone, especially romantically. *Example:* She felt he was leading her on with his mixed signals. *Example:* He didn't want to lead her on if he wasn't interested.

25 LEAD THE WAY

Meaning: To show others the correct path or method.

Example: She led the way in implementing the new procedures. *Example:* The pioneering scientist led the way in cancer research.

26 LEAN ON

Meaning: To rely on someone for support.

Example: During tough times, she leaned on her friends.

Example: He leaned on his mentor for advice.

27 LEARN BY HEART

Meaning: To memorize something perfectly.

Example: She learned the poem by heart for the recital.

Example: He learned all the definitions by heart.

28 LEARN THE ROPES

Meaning: To understand how to do a job or activity.

Example: It took her a few weeks to learn the ropes at her new job. *Example:* He quickly learned the ropes of the software.

29 LEAVE A BAD TASTE IN ONE'S MOUTH

Meaning: To leave a negative impression or feeling.

Example: The rude service left a bad taste in her mouth.

Example: His dishonesty left a bad taste in everyone's mouth.

30 LEAVE HIGH AND DRY

Meaning: To abandon someone in a difficult situation.

Example: The sudden resignation left the team high and dry. *Example:* She felt left high and dry when her partner quit.

31 LEAVE NO STONE UNTURNED

Meaning: To try every possible way to achieve something. *Example:* They left no stone unturned in their search for the missing dog.

Example: She left no stone unturned in preparing for the exam.

32 LEAVE SOMEONE IN THE LURCH

Meaning: To abandon someone in a difficult situation without help. *Example:* He left her in the lurch just when she needed him most. *Example:* The sudden strike left the company in the lurch.

33 LEAVE WELL ENOUGH ALONE

Meaning: To avoid changing something that is satisfactory. *Example:* The project is going well; let's leave well enough alone. *Example:* She decided to leave well enough alone instead of making more changes.

34 LEND AN EAR

Meaning: To listen carefully and sympathetically.

Example: He always lends an ear to his friend's problems.

Example: She was grateful to anyone who would lend an ear during her tough times.

35 LEND A HAND

Meaning: To help someone.

Example: Can you lend a hand with these boxes?

Example: She lent a hand in organizing the event.

36 LET BYGONES BE BYGONES

Meaning: To forget past disagreements and move on.

Example: They decided to let bygones be bygones and reconcile. *Example:* It's time to let bygones be bygones and focus on the future.

37 LET DOWN EASY

Meaning: To reject someone gently.

Example: She let him down easy when he asked her out.

Example: He tried to let her down easy about the job rejection.

38 LET OFF STEAM

Meaning: To release pent-up energy or emotion.

Example: He ran to let off steam after the argument. *Example:* She likes to let off steam by playing the drums.

39 LET ONE'S HAIR DOWN

Meaning: To relax and enjoy oneself.

Example: She decided to let her hair down and go dancing. *Example:* The students let their hair down after the exams and celebrated.

40 LET SLEEPING DOGS LIE

Meaning: To avoid stirring up trouble by leaving a situation alone. *Example:* He decided to let sleeping dogs lie and not mention the argument.

Example: Sometimes, it's best to let sleeping dogs lie and not revisit old issues.

41 LET THE CHIPS FALL WHERE THEY MAY

Meaning: To allow events to unfold naturally without trying to control them.

Example: She decided to tell the truth and let the chips fall where they may.

Example: He decided to let the chips fall where they may.

42 LETTER PERFECT

Meaning: Completely accurate or precise.

Example: Her performance was letter perfect.

Example: He delivered a letter-perfect speech.

43 LEVEL PLAYING FIELD

Meaning: A situation where everyone has an equal chance of success.

Example: The new rules created a level playing field for all participants.

Example: They aim to provide a level playing field for all employees.

44 LEVEL WITH

Meaning: To be honest or straightforward with someone.

Example: He decided to level with his boss about his concerns.

Example: She leveled with her friend about the situation.

45 LIE THROUGH ONE'S TEETH

Meaning: To lie boldly and shamelessly.

Example: He lied through his teeth to avoid getting into trouble.

Example: She knew he was lying through his teeth but couldn't prove it.

46 LIFE IN THE FAST LANE

Meaning: A way of living that is full of excitement and activity.

Example: He enjoys life in the fast lane with his high-powered job.

Example: She decided to slow down after years of life in the fast lane.

47 LIGHT A FIRE UNDER SOMEONE

Meaning: To motivate someone to take action.

Example: The deadline lit a fire under him to finish the project.

Example: She tried to light a fire under her team to meet their targets.

48 LIGHT AT THE END OF THE TUNNEL

Meaning: Signs of improvement in a difficult situation.

Example: After months of hard work, they finally saw light at the end of the tunnel.

Example: She felt there was light at the end of the tunnel after her recovery.

49 LIGHT BULB MOMENT

Meaning: A moment of sudden realization or understanding.

Example: She had a light bulb moment and solved the problem.

Example: The discussion led to a light bulb moment for the team.

50 LIGHT ON ONE'S FEET

Meaning: To be agile and quick in movement.

Example: The dancer was light on her feet.

Example: He needs to be light on his feet to play soccer well.

51 LIGHT YEARS

Meaning: Very far ahead in development or progress.

Example: The new technology is light years ahead of the old one.

Example: His ideas are light years ahead of his time.

52 LIGHTEN THE LOAD

Meaning: To make a task or burden easier to handle.

Example: They hired extra help to lighten the load.

Example: Sharing the work helped to lighten the load for everyone.

53 LIKE A BROKEN RECORD

Meaning: Repeating the same thing over and over again.

Example: He sounds like a broken record with his constant complaints.

Example: She's like a broken record, always discussing the same problems.

54 LIKE A FISH OUT OF WATER

Meaning: Feeling uncomfortable or out of place in a situation.

Example: At the formal event, he felt like a fish out of water.

Example: She was like a fish out of water in her new job.

55 LIKE A KID IN A CANDY STORE

Meaning: Very excited and happy about something.

Example: He was like a kid in a candy store when he saw the new gadgets.

Example: She felt like a kid in a candy store at the fashion show.

56 LIKE CLOCKWORK

Meaning: Happening regularly or precisely.

Example: The train runs like clockwork every morning.

Example: The project progressed like clockwork, meeting every deadline.

57 LIKE PULLING TEETH

Meaning: Very difficult or unpleasant to do.

Example: Getting him to talk about his feelings is like pulling teeth.

Example: Convincing her to try new foods is like pulling teeth.

58 LIKE TAKING CANDY FROM A BABY

Meaning: Very easy to do.

Example: The test was so simple; it was like taking candy from a baby.

Example: Winning the game was like taking candy from a baby.

59 LIKE THE BACK OF ONE'S HAND

Meaning: Very familiar with something.

Example: She knows the city like the back of her hand.

Example: He knows the software like the back of his hand.

60 LIKE THERE'S NO TOMORROW

Meaning: Doing something with great intensity or urgency.

Example: They partied like there was no tomorrow.

Example: She worked like there was no tomorrow to finish the project.

61 LIKE WATER OFF A DUCK'S BACK

Meaning: Not affected by criticism or negative comments.

Example: The insults were like water off a duck's back to him.

Example: She let the criticism slide off her like water off a duck's back.

62 LILY-LIVERED

Meaning: Cowardly or lacking in courage.

Example: He was too lily-livered to stand up for himself.

Example: She called him lily-livered for not confronting the issue.

63 LION'S SHARE

Meaning: The largest part or most of something.

Example: He took the lion's share of the credit for the project.

Example: The lion's share of the budget was allocated to marketing.

64 LIP SERVICE

Meaning: Insincere expression of respect.

Example: The company paid lip service to environmental issues but did little.

Example: He gave lip service to the idea but never acted on it.

65 LITTLE BY LITTLE

Meaning: Gradually; step by step.

Example: She improved little by little with daily practice.

Example: Little by little, they built their business.

66 LIVE AND LEARN

Meaning: To learn from one's experiences.

Example: I didn't realize that would happen, but you live and learn.

Example: She made a mistake, but she'll live and learn from it.

67 LIVE AND LET LIVE

Meaning: To accept and tolerate differences.

Example: They have a live-and-let-live attitude in their community.

Example: She believes in live and let live, not interfering with others' choices.

68 LIVE IN A BUBBLE

Meaning: To be isolated from the real world or unaware of reality.

Example: He lives in a bubble, unaware of the struggles others face.

Example: They lived in a bubble, thinking everything was perfect.

Live in a bubble

69 LIVE IN THE FAST LANE

Meaning: To live a lifestyle characterized by excitement and risk.

Example: He's been living in the fast lane since he moved to the city.

Example: She enjoys living in the fast lane with her adventurous activities.

70 LIVE THE DREAM

Meaning: Experiencing a life or situation that one has always desired or aspired to, often implying that everything is going exceptionally well.

Example: After years of hard work and saving, Maria finally opened her own bakery. Now, she spends her days surrounded by delicious pastries and happy customers—she's truly living the dream.

Example: Mark travels the world as a professional photographer, capturing stunning landscapes and meeting new people daily. For him, it's living the dream.

71 LIVE UP TO

Meaning: To meet or equal expectations or standards.

Example: The movie didn't live up to the hype.

Example: He strives to live up to his parents' expectations.

72 LIVING ON BORROWED TIME

Meaning: Existing precariously, with the possibility of imminent failure or death.

Example: After the surgery, he felt like he was living on borrowed time.

Example: The company is living on borrowed time unless it finds new investors.

73 LOADED QUESTION

Meaning: a question that contains a presumption or implies something that forces the respondent to agree with an assumption they may not believe in. It often leads the person answering the question into a trap, making it difficult to respond without conceding to the implied point.

Example: During the interview, she was asked a loaded question about her previous employer, which made it difficult for her to answer without sounding critical.

Example: When asked, *"Why do you always avoid taking responsibility?"* he realized it was a loaded question designed to make him look bad regardless of his answer

74 LOCK HORNS

Meaning: To engage in conflict or argument.

Example: The two politicians often lock horns over policy issues.

Example: They locked horns during the meeting, each defending their own view.

75 LOCK, STOCK, AND BARREL

Meaning: Everything; the whole thing.

Example: They sold the business lock, stock, and barrel.

Example: He bought the collection lock, stock, and barrel.

76 LONG IN THE TOOTH

Meaning: Old or getting old.

Example: He's getting a bit long in the tooth for this kind of work.

Example: The car is long in the tooth but still runs well.

77 LOOSE CANNON

Meaning: An unpredictable person who may cause damage if not controlled.

Example: He's a loose cannon and often says things that get him into trouble.

Example: The new employee is a bit of a loose cannon but also very creative.

78 LOSE HEART

Meaning: To become discouraged or lose confidence in something, especially when facing difficulties or challenges.

Example: After several failed attempts to pass the exam, Sarah began to *lose heart*, wondering if she would ever succeed.

Example: The team started to lose heart when it fell behind by three goals, but their coach motivated them to keep fighting until the end.

79 LOSE ONE'S HEAD

Meaning: To become very upset or angry.

Example: He lost his head when he found out about the betrayal.

Example: She tends to lose her head during stressful situations.

80 LOSE ONE'S MARBLES

Meaning: To go crazy or lose one's mind.

Example: He thought he was losing his marbles after working non-stop for days.

Example: She felt like she was losing her marbles during the hectic move.

81 LOSE TRACK OF TIME

Meaning: To become unaware of the time and miss deadlines or appointments.

Example: She lost track of time while reading and missed her appointment.

Example: He often loses track of time when he's playing video games.

82 LOSE TOUCH

Meaning: To fail to keep in contact with someone.

Example: They lost touch after college but reconnected years later.

Example: She lost touch with her old friends after moving away.

83 LOST CAUSE

Meaning: A hopeless situation or case.

Example: Trying to fix that old car is a lost cause.

Example: She realized the relationship was a lost cause and decided to move on.

84 LOUD AND CLEAR

Meaning: Very clear and easy to understand.

Example: The message came through loud and clear.

Example: She heard him loud and clear and knew exactly what he meant.

85 LOVE AT FIRST SIGHT

Meaning: An immediate and strong attraction to someone upon first seeing them.

Example: It was love at first sight when they met at the party.

Example: He believes in love at first sight and hopes to experience it one day.

86 LOVE HANDLES

Meaning: Extra fat around the waist.

Example: He's been exercising to get rid of his love handles.

Example: She embraced her love handles and felt confident in her body.

87 LOW-HANGING FRUIT

Meaning: The easiest targets or tasks.

Example: Let's start with the low-hanging fruit before tackling the more complex issues.

Example: The team focused on the low-hanging fruit to achieve quick results.

88 LOW-KEY

Meaning: Quiet, modest, or understated.

Example: They had a low-key celebration with just close friends.

Example: She prefers low-key events over big parties.

89 LOOK A GIFT HORSE IN THE MOUTH

Meaning: To find fault with something received as a gift or favor.

Example: Don't look a gift horse in the mouth; be grateful for what you have.

Example: He looked a gift horse in the mouth and complained about the free meal.

90 LOOK BEFORE YOU LEAP

Meaning: To think carefully before taking action.

Example: She should look before she leaps into a new job.

Example: He didn't look before he leaped and now regrets his decision.

91 LOOK DOWN ONE'S NOSE AT

Meaning: To regard with disdain or contempt.

Example: She looks down her nose at anyone who doesn't have a degree.

Example: He looked down his nose at their humble beginnings.

92 LOOK LIKE A MILLION DOLLARS

Meaning: To look very attractive or impressive.

Example: She looked like a million dollars in her new dress.

Example: He felt like a million dollars after the makeover.

93 LOOK ON THE BRIGHT SIDE

Meaning: To find the positive aspects of a situation.

Example: Even after losing the game, he tried to look on the bright side.

Example: She always looks on the bright side of things, no matter how bad they are.

94 LOOK THE OTHER WAY

Meaning: To ignore something that one should not overlook.

Example: The teacher looked the other way when the student was cheating.

Example: She decided to look the other way and not report the minor infraction.

95 LOOK THE PART

Meaning: To appear suitable for a particular role or situation.

Example: He dressed in a sharp suit to look the part for the interview.

Example: She looked the part of a professional chef in her new uniform.

96 LOOK UP TO

Meaning: To admire or respect someone.

Example: She looks up to her older sister.

Example: Many people look up to him as a leader.

97 LUCKY BREAK

Meaning: A fortunate or unexpected turn of events.

Example: He got a lucky break when he found a new job right after being laid off.

Example: Her lucky break came when she won the scholarship.

98 LUMP IN ONE'S THROAT

Meaning: A feeling of tightness or a sensation as if there is something in one's throat, usually due to strong emotion, often sadness or overwhelming happiness.

Example: She felt a lump in her throat as she watched her son walk across the stage to receive his diploma.

Example: During the farewell speech, he had a lump in his throat, struggling to hold back tears.

99 LYING THROUGH ONE'S TEETH

Meaning: To lie blatantly.

Example: She knew he was lying through his teeth about his alibi.

Example: He was lying through his teeth to get out of trouble.

100 LUST FOR LIFE

Meaning: A strong passion or enthusiasm for living, often characterized by a zestful, energetic, and adventurous attitude toward life.

Example: Her lust for life was evident in her constant travel and pursuit of new experiences, always eager to explore and learn.

Example: Despite his challenges, his lust for life never faded, inspiring those around him with his boundless energy and optimism.

* * *

ACTIVITY 4

Please fill in the blanks with the idioms in italics below:

Lena had always _____1_____, no matter what life threw at her. But when she unexpectedly lost her job, even she found it hard to keep her spirits up. "Sometimes, you just have to _____2_____," she told herself, trying to stay positive.

With her savings dwindling, Lena decided it was time to _____3_____of freelancing. At first, it was _____4_____—clients were hard to come by, and the competition was fierce. But Lena was determined not to_____5_____. She knew that if she _____6_____ and gave it her all, something good would eventually come her way.

After months of hard work, Lena finally landed a big project. It was _____7_____, and she felt like she was _____8_____. As she signed the contract, she couldn't help but think, "This might have been a tough journey, but I'm glad I didn't _____9_____in pursuing this new path."

* * *

looked on the bright side

let the chips fall where they may

learn the ropes

like pulling teeth

lose heart

lived as if there was no tomorrow

light at the end of the tunnel,

living the dream

leave no stone unturned

A RECAP OF IDIOMS LEARNT: CAN YOU GUESS THE MEANING OF THESE SENTENCES?

- He was learning the ropes quickly but knew he had to let sleeping dogs lie to avoid unnecessary conflicts.
- She had to lay it on the line during the meeting, knowing it was now or never to lock in the deal.

Need more help? Connect with A M Lucas for the option of one-on-one coaching.

IDIOMS BEGINNING WITH M

*H*ere's the 100

1 MAD AS A HATTER

Meaning: someone who is very eccentric, crazy, or behaving unusually or irrationally.

Example: Everyone thought the inventor was mad as a hatter for trying to build a flying car, but he was determined to prove them wrong.

Example: The old man down the street is mad as a hatter; he spends his days talking to his garden gnomes as if they were real people.

2 MAGIC MOMENT

Meaning: A special, memorable, or enchanting moment.

Example: Their first kiss was a magic moment they'll never forget.

Example: The magic moment of the night was when the fireworks started.

3 MAGIC TOUCH

Meaning: An exceptional ability to achieve positive results.

Example: She has a magic touch when it comes to gardening.

Example: His magic touch with children made him a beloved teacher.

4 MAGNETIC PERSONALITY

Meaning: A very charming and attractive personality that draws others in.

Example: Her magnetic personality made her the center of attention at every party.

Example: He had a magnetic personality that attracted many followers.

5 MAKE A BEELINE FOR

Meaning: To go directly toward something or someone.

Example: She made a beeline for the dessert table as soon as she entered the party.

Example: He made a beeline for the exit during the meeting.

6 MAKE A CASE FOR SOMETHING

Meaning: To provide arguments or reasons in support of something.

Example: The lawyer made a strong case for his client's innocence.

Example: She made a case to extend the deadline.

7 MAKE A CLEAN BREAST OF

Meaning: To confess something.

Example: He made a clean breast of his involvement in the scheme.

Example: She decided to make a clean breast of her mistakes.

8 MAKE A KILLING

Meaning: To make a significant profit.

Example: She made a killing by investing in real estate.

Example: They made a killing at the stock market.

9 MAKE A LONG STORY SHORT

Meaning: To summarize a lengthy story.

Example: To make a long story short, we missed the flight.

Example: To make a long story short, they decided not to buy the house.

10 MAKE A MOUNTAIN OUT OF A MOLEHILL

Meaning: To exaggerate a minor problem.

Example: She's making a mountain out of a molehill by worrying about that small mistake.

Example: Don't make a mountain out of a molehill; it's just a minor issue.

11 MAKE A NAME FOR ONESELF

Meaning: To become well-known or famous.

Example: He made a name for himself in the tech industry.

Example: She's made a name for herself as a talented artist.

12 MAKE A POINT OF

Meaning: To intentionally make an effort to do something.

Example: He made a point of thanking everyone for their hard work.

Example: She makes a point of exercising every day.3

Meaning: To attempt to escape quickly.

Example: The prisoners made a run for it during the guard change.

Example: He made a run for it when he saw the police.

14 MAKE A SCENE

Meaning: To create a loud, noticeable disturbance.

Example: She made a scene when she found out her order was wrong.

Example: He doesn't like to make a scene in public.

15 MAKE A SPLASH

Meaning: To attract a lot of attention.

Example: Her debut film made a splash at the festival.

Example: The new restaurant made a splash with its unique menu.

16 MAKE AMENDS

Meaning: To apologize and fix a mistake.

Example: He tried to make amends for his rudeness.

Example: She made amends by helping her friend with the project.

17 MAKE AN EXAMPLE OF

Meaning: To punish someone in a way that serves as a warning to others.

Example: The teacher made an example of the student who cheated on the test by giving him detention.

Example: The manager deducted a day's pay to make an example of the employee who was consistently late.

16 MAKE AN EXCEPTION

Meaning: To treat someone or something as a special case.

Example: The teacher made an exception and allowed the student to submit the assignment late.

Example: Can you make an exception just this once?

19 MAKE BELIEVE

Meaning: Pretend; fantasy.

Example: The children played a game of make believe, pretending to be pirates.

Example: Her stories were filled with make believe and adventure.

20 MAKE BOTH ENDS MEET

Meaning: To manage financially, especially with difficulty, weighing two situations.

Example: After losing his job, he took on two part-time positions to make both ends meet.

Example: With rising expenses and the loss of his job, it's become hard for his family to make both ends meet.

21 MAKE ENDS MEET

Meaning: To manage financially.

Example: It's hard to make ends meet on a low salary.

Example: They struggled to make ends meet after losing their jobs.

22 MAKE HEADWAY

Meaning: To make progress.

Example: We're finally making headway on the project.

Example: She made headway in her studies after hiring a tutor.

23 MAKE HAY WHILE THE SUN SHINES

Meaning: To take advantage of an opportunity while it lasts.

Example: You should make hay while the sun shines and finish your work while you have the energy.

Example: They decided to make hay while the sun shines and sell their house at a high price.

24 MAKE IT UP TO SOMEONE

Meaning: To do something good for someone to compensate for a wrongdoing.

Example: He apologized and promised to make it up to her.

Example: She made it up to him by cooking his favorite meal.

25 MAKE LIGHT OF

Meaning: To treat something as less serious than it is.

Example: He made light of the situation to keep everyone calm.

Example: Don't make light of her concerns; they are valid.

26 MAKE NO BONES ABOUT

Meaning: To be open and honest about something.

Example: She made no bones about her dislike for the new policy.

Example: He made no bones about his desire to leave the company.

27 MAKE ONE'S BED AND LIE IN IT

Meaning: To accept the consequences of one's actions.

Example: You've made your bed; now you have to lie in it.

Example: She realized she had to make her bed and lie in it after making that decision.

28 MAKE ONE'S BLOOD BOIL

Meaning: To make someone very angry.

Example: His arrogant attitude makes my blood boil.

Example: The injustice of the situation made her blood boil.

29 MAKE ONE'S DAY

Meaning: To make someone very happy.

Example: Her compliment made my day.

Example: The surprise visit made his day.

30 MAKE ONE'S MOUTH WATER

Meaning: To cause someone to salivate in anticipation of delicious food.

Example: The aroma of the baking bread made my mouth water.

Example: The sight of the dessert made his mouth water.

31 MAKE ONE'S WAY

Meaning: To move or progress, often with effort.

Example: He made his way through the crowded room.

Example: She made her way to the top of the company.

32 MAKE OR BREAK

Meaning: To be the deciding factor in success or failure.

Example: The next project could make or break his career.

Example: It's a make-or-break moment for the company.

33 MAKE SHORT WORK OF

Meaning: To finish something quickly and easily.

Example: She did short work on the assignment.

Example: The team made short work of the project.

35 MAKE THE CUT

Meaning: To meet the required standard.

Example: She practiced hard to make the cut for the soccer team.

Example: Only a few candidates made the cut for the final interview.

36 MAKE THE GRADE

Meaning: To meet the required standard.

Example: He worked hard to make the grade in his exams.

Example: She didn't make the grade for the advanced class.

37 MAKE THE MOST OF SOMETHING

Meaning: To take full advantage of something.

Example: She made the most of her time in the city by visiting all the museums.

Example: He made the most of the opportunity to learn from his mentor.

38 MAKE THE ROUNDS

Meaning: To go from place to place, especially as part of a routine.

Example: The doctor made the rounds at the hospital.

Example: The rumor quickly made the rounds around the office.

39 MAKE TIME FOR

Meaning: To schedule time to do something.

Example: She always makes time for her family, no matter how busy she is.

Example: He made time for exercise in his daily routine.

40 MAKE TOO MUCH OF SOMETHING

Meaning: To exaggerate the importance or seriousness of something.

Example: He's making too much of the mistake; it's not a big deal.

Example: Don't make too much of her comments; she was just joking.

41 MAKE UP FOR LOST TIME

Meaning: To compensate for lost opportunities.

Example: They worked extra hours to make up for lost time.

Example: She spent the weekend studying to make up for lost time.

42 MAKE WAVES

Meaning: To cause disruption or controversy.

Example: His radical ideas made waves in the company.

Example: She tends to make waves with her outspoken opinions.

43 MAKE YOUR BLOOD RUN COLD

Meaning: To cause someone to feel intense fear.

Example: The ghost story made my blood run cold.

Example: The news of the attack made her blood run cold.

44 MAKE YOUR MARK

Meaning: To achieve something notable or make a significant impact.

Example: He made his mark in the film industry with his first blockbuster.

Example: She made her mark as a leading scientist in the field of genetics.

45 MAKE YOURSELF HEARD/UNDERSTOOD/KNOWN

Meaning: To ensure that others hear, understand, or recognize you.

Example: He made himself heard over the noisy crowd.

Example: She made herself understood despite the language barrier.

Example: He made himself known as a talented artist in the community.

46 MANAGE A FEW WORDS

Meaning: To speak, often with difficulty or effort.

Example: He managed a few words despite his nervousness.

Example: She managed a few words of thanks before breaking down in tears.

47 MAN IN THE STREET

Meaning: An average or typical person.

Example: The survey asked the opinion of the man in the street.

Example: His views represent those of the man in the street.

48 MAN OF FEW WORDS

Meaning: A person who speaks very little but is often thoughtful or impactful when they do.

Example: Despite being a man of few words, his speech at the event was deeply moving.

Example: He's a man of few words, but his actions always speak louder than his words.

49 MAN OF HIS WORD

Meaning: Someone who keeps promises and is trustworthy.

Example: He's a man of his word; you can count on him.

Example: She knew he was a man of his word and trusted him completely.

50 MANDATE TO DO SOMETHING

Meaning: An official order or commission to do something.

Example: The committee has a mandate to investigate the issue.

Example: The government issued a mandate to reduce carbon emissions.

51 MANIPULATE SOMEBODY INTO DOING SOMETHING

Meaning: To influence or control someone to do something, often in a deceitful way.

Example: He manipulated her into signing the contract.

Example: She was manipulated into making a donation she couldn't afford.

52 MANIFEST SOMETHING IN/AS/THROUGH SOMETHING

Meaning: To show or demonstrate something clearly through actions or signs.

Example: His talent manifested itself in his paintings.

Example: Her leadership skills manifested as she led the team through the crisis.

53 MANNER OF (DOING) SOMETHING

Meaning: The way in which something is done.

Example: His manner of speaking was very formal.

Example: The manner of solving the problem was innovative.

54 MANY HAPPY RETURNS

Meaning: A phrase used to wish someone a happy birthday.

Example: Many happy returns on your special day!

Example: We hope you have many happy returns of the day.

55 MANY HANDS MAKE LIGHT WORK

Meaning: Tasks become easier when many people work together.

Example: We finished the project quickly because many hands make light work.

Example: The cleanup was done in no time because many hands make light work.

56 MARGIN FOR ERROR

Meaning: The amount of leeway allowed for mistakes or inaccuracies.

Example: There's very little margin for error in this high-stakes project.

Example: The engineers built in a margin for error to ensure safety.

57 MARKED MAN/WOMAN

Meaning: Someone who is singled out for special attention, often negative.

Example: After his testimony, he became a marked man.

Example: She felt like a marked woman after standing up to the boss.

58 MARK MY WORDS

Meaning: Pay attention to what I'm saying because it will happen.

Example: Mark my words, you'll regret this decision.

Example: She told him to mark her words about the consequences.

59 MARK TIME

Meaning: To wait or be inactive.

Example: He was marking time until his next job started.

Example: They marked time while waiting for the meeting to begin.

60 MARKET SOMETHING FOR SOMEBODY

Meaning: To promote or sell a product or service on behalf of someone.

Example: The company is marketing the new software for a tech startup.

Example: She was hired to market the handmade jewelry for a local artisan.

61 MASSES OF SOMETHING

Meaning: A large quantity or a huge amount of something.

Example: There were masses of people at the concert, making it difficult to find a spot to sit.

Example: She has masses of paperwork to complete before the deadline.

62 MASSAGE SOMEBODY'S EGO

Meaning: To flatter or praise someone to make them feel better about themselves or to boost their confidence.

Example: During the meeting, she massaged his ego by complimenting his leadership skills.

Example: The coach massaged the team's ego after the loss, reminding them of their previous successes.

63 MASSIVE ROW/ARGUMENT

Meaning: A very intense or heated disagreement or fight.

Example: There was a massive row between the neighbors over the property boundaries.

Example: The couple had a massive argument about finances, but they resolved it later.

64 MASTER OF YOUR OWN FATE

Meaning: To be in control of your own life and decisions, taking responsibility for your success or failure.

Example: She believes that with hard work and determination, you can become the master of your own fate.

Example: By starting his own business, he decided to be the master of his own fate rather than depend on a traditional job.

65 MATTER OF FACT

Meaning: Something that is true and cannot be disputed.

Example: As a matter of fact, I have the documents right here.

Example: He spoke in a matter-of-fact tone.

66 MATTER-OF-FACT VOICE/TONE

Meaning: Speaking in a calm, unemotional, and straightforward manner, often without showing strong feelings or opinions.

Example: She explained the situation in a matter-of-fact tone, even though it was a serious issue.

Example: His matter-of-fact voice while describing the accident made it seem less dramatic.

67 MATTER OF LIFE AND DEATH

Meaning: A situation or issue of extreme importance or urgency, often involving survival or serious consequences.

Example: Getting the injured man to the hospital quickly was a matter of life and death.

Example: To her, the decision to save the family business felt like a matter of life and death.

68 MAY AS WELL

Meaning: Used to suggest that something should be done because there is no better alternative or because it is practical under the circumstances.

Example: Since we're already here, we may as well check out the museum.

Example: There's no bus for another hour, so we may as well walk to the station.

69 MAY WELL

Meaning: Used to express that something is likely or has a good chance of happening.

Example: If we keep working hard, we may well finish the project ahead of schedule.

Example: Given the weather forecast, it may well rain this afternoon.

70 ME TIME

Meaning: Time spent relaxing or doing things for oneself, especially to recharge or take a break from responsibilities.

Example: After a busy week at work, she dedicated Sunday to some much-needed me time.

Example: Taking a walk in the park is his favorite way to enjoy some me time.

71 ME NEITHER

Meaning: A way to agree with a negative statement or express that the same applies to oneself.

Example: Person A: "I don't like spicy food."

Person B: "Me neither. I can't handle the heat."

Example: Person A: "I haven't seen that movie yet."

Person B: "Me neither. Let's watch it together."

72 MEAGRE INCOME/EARNINGS/WAGES

Meaning: A very small or insufficient amount of money earned or received, often barely enough to live on.

Example: Despite working long hours, she struggled to support her family on her meager income.

Example: Many workers protested against the company for paying such meager wages.

73 MEET HALFWAY

Meaning: To compromise with someone.

Example: They agreed to meet halfway and split the costs.

Example: She decided to meet him halfway to resolve their differences.

74 MEN IN GREY SUITS

Meaning: Powerful businessmen or bureaucrats, often seen as conservative and anonymous.

Example: The decision was made by the men in grey suits at the headquarters.

Example: She often clashed with the men in grey suits over her creative ideas.

75 MEND FENCES

Meaning: To repair a relationship.

Example: After their argument, they decided to mend fences.

Example: She wants to mend fences with her estranged brother.

76 METHOD TO THE MADNESS

Meaning: A reason for someone's strange behavior.

Example: His desk may look chaotic, but there's a method to his madness.

Example: There seems to be a method to her madness in how she organizes things.

77 MIND YOUR OWN BUSINESS

Meaning: To focus on your own affairs and not interfere with others.

Example: When he asked about her plans, she told him to mind his own business.

Example: I suggest you mind your own business and stop meddling.

78 MIND YOUR PS AND QS

Meaning: To be careful about what you say and do.

Example: During the field trip, the teacher reminded the students to mind their Ps and Qs.

Example: He always minds his Ps and Qs in front of his boss.

79 MISS THE BOAT

Meaning: To miss an opportunity.

Example: He missed the boat by not investing in the company early on.

Example: She realized she had missed the boat when the deadline passed.

80 MISS THE MARK

Meaning: To fail to achieve the intended result.

Example: The advertisement missed the mark with the target audience.

Example: His attempt at humor missed the mark and offended people.

81 MOMENT OF TRUTH

Meaning: A critical or decisive time when one is put to the test.

Example: The moment of truth came when he had to present his findings.

Example: She faced the moment of truth during the final interview.

82 MONEY TALKS

Meaning: Money has the power to influence people and decisions.

Example: In politics, money talks and can sway decisions.

Example: He believes that money talks in the business world.

83 MORE THAN MEETS THE EYE

Meaning: Something is more complex than it appears.

Example: There's more to this problem than meets the eye.

Example: She suspected there was more to the story than meets the eye.

84 MOUTH-WATERING

Meaning: Delicious or appetizing.

Example: The bakery display was full of mouth-watering pastries.

Example: The aroma from the kitchen was mouth-watering.

85 MOVE HEAVEN AND EARTH

Meaning: To do everything possible to achieve something.

Example: He moved heaven and earth to get his project approved.

Example: She would move heaven and earth to help her family.

Move heaven and earth

86 MOVE MOUNTAINS

Meaning: To achieve something difficult.

Example: With enough determination, you can move mountains.

Example: She moved mountains to get her business off the ground.

87 MOVE THE GOALPOSTS

Meaning: To change the criteria or rules in a situation, making it more difficult.

Example: It's frustrating when they keep moving the goalposts.

Example: They moved the goalposts by adding new requirements.

88 MOVE UP IN THE WORLD

Meaning: To achieve a higher level of status or success.

Example: She's been moving up in the world since she got that promotion.

Example: He moved up in the world after starting his own business.

89 MUCH ADO ABOUT NOTHING

Meaning: A lot of fuss over something unimportant.

Example: Their argument was much ado about nothing.

Example: The controversy turned out to be much ado about nothing.

90 MUDDY THE WATERS

Meaning: To make a situation more confusing.

Example: His contradictory statements muddied the waters.

Example: The additional information only muddied the waters.

91 MUD-SLINGING

Meaning: The act of making malicious or scandalous allegations about an opponent.

Example: The election campaign was full of mud-slinging.

Example: She refused to engage in mud-slinging during the debate.

92 MULL OVER SOMETHING

Meaning: To think carefully about something before making a decision.

Example: She needed some time to mull over the job offer before accepting it.

Example: He spent the weekend mulling over the best strategy for the project.

93 MUM'S THE WORD

Meaning: To keep something secret.

Example: Mum's the word about the surprise party.

Example: He told them mum's the word regarding the new project.

94 MUSIC TO ONE'S EARS

Meaning: Something that is very pleasing to hear.

Example: The news of her promotion was music to her ears.

Example: His compliment was music to her ears.

95 MUSTER UP

Meaning: To gather or summon up (courage, energy, etc.).

Example: He mustered up the courage to ask her out.

Example: She mustered up the energy to finish the marathon.

96 MUTUAL AGREEMENT/CONSENT

Meaning: A decision or arrangement made together by all parties involved, with everyone's approval.

Example: The contract was terminated by mutual agreement between the employer and the employee.

Example: They decided to end their partnership by mutual consent, with no hard feelings.

97 MY HANDS ARE TIED

Meaning: Unable to act due to restrictions or constraints.

Example: I wish I could help, but my hands are tied.

Example: Her hands were tied due to the company's policies.

98 MY HEART GOES OUT TO

Meaning: To feel sympathy for someone.

Example: My heart goes out to the families of the victims.

Example: His heart went out to her during her time of loss.

99 MY TWO CENTS

Meaning: One's opinion or contribution to a discussion.

Example: If I could add my two cents, I think we should go with the first option.

Example: He offered his two cents on the issue during the meeting.

100 MY WAY OR THE HIGHWAY

Meaning: An ultimatum meaning that one must either accept what is offered or leave.

Example: The boss's attitude was my way or the highway.

Example: During negotiations, he told them it was his way or the highway.

* * *

ACTIVITY 5

Please fill in the blanks with the idioms in italics below:

Max had always been _____1_____, but when he spoke, people listened. He had a reputation for _____2_____ when it came to his creative ideas, but that's what made him such a valuable member of the team. His latest project was no different—_____3_____, as they called it. The entire company was depending on its success.

Despite the pressure, Max stayed cool as a cucumber. He knew that _____4_____ wouldn't help anyone, so he kept things in perspective and encouraged his team to do the same. They worked morning, noon, and night; there was _____5_____ to prepare everything for the big presentation.

When the day finally arrived, Max took a deep breath and _____6_____ for the conference room. The presentation _____7_____, and the clients were impressed. It was clear that all their hard work had paid off. As they celebrated, Max couldn't help but feel proud. He had _____8_____ to make this happen, and now, he could finally take a moment to relax.

* * *

a man of few words

making short work

make or break

making a mountain out of a molehill

no margin for error

made a beeline

made the grade

moved heaven and earth

A RECAP OF IDIOMS LEARNT: CAN YOU GUESS AT THE MEANING OF THESE SENTENCES?

- He made a mountain out of a molehill, stressing over something that wasn't worth the trouble.
- We need to mend fences with the client to maintain a good relationship moving forward.

You can contact A. M. Lucas for one-on-one coaching. For more information, see the Afterword at the end of the book.

TAKE A MOMENT...

Help Others on Their English Learning Journey: Review this book.

> The best way to find yourself is to lose yourself in the service of others." – Mahatma Gandhi

When we take a moment to help someone else, we're doing something powerful. It feels good, right? And it doesn't take much time or effort. Now, I have a simple favor to ask you...

Would you help someone you've never met if it took less than a minute, and all it cost you was kindness?

That someone is a person just like you were. They want to improve their English, to sound more natural and confident, but they don't know where to start.

Our goal is to make English idioms easy and fun for everyone. We want people all over the world to feel confident when they speak and write in English, no matter where they are. The best way for us to help more people is by spreading the word, and that's where you come in.

Most people really do judge a book by its cover—and its reviews! So here's what I'm asking, on behalf of someone just starting their English journey:

Please leave a review of this book.

Your review costs nothing and takes less than 60 seconds. Your words might help...

...one more student understand common English phrases.

...one more worker sound more fluent at their job.

...one more traveler make friends across the world.

...one more learner feel more confident every day.

To help someone else with their English, all you have to do is leave a review. It's that simple.

How to Leave a Review:

- On Amazon: Scroll to the bottom of the book's page and click "Write a Customer Review."

- On Goodreads: Head to the book's page, and click "Write a Review."

- or click here https://www.amazon.com/review/review-your-purchases/?asin=BOOKASIN

-or click on the QR code below

* * *

* * *

Thank you so much for your support. Your review means a lot, and I can't wait to continue helping you master English idioms.

- Your biggest fan,

A M Lucas

PS – Fun fact: Helping others feels great! If you know someone else who's learning English, why not share this book with them? You might just change their life too!

IDIOMS BEGINNING WITH N

*H*ere's the 100

1 NAIL IN THE COFFIN

Meaning: An action or event that will likely lead to failure or demise.

Example: The scandal was the final nail in the coffin of his political career.

Example: Losing the contract was a nail in the coffin for the struggling company.

2 NAIL-BITER

Meaning: A situation causing intense suspense or anxiety.

Example: The game was a real nail-biter until the final whistle.

Example: Waiting for the test results was a nail-biter.

3 NAIL IT

Meaning: To do something perfectly or successfully.

Example: She nailed her presentation at the conference.

Example: He nailed the audition and got the part.

4 NAIL SOMETHING DOWN

Meaning: To finalize or make something definite.

Example: We need to nail down the details of the contract.

Example: They nailed down the date for the event.

5 NAKED EYE

Meaning: Without the use of any devices such as telescopes or microscopes.

Example: The comet was visible to the naked eye.

Example: The damage was not visible to the naked eye.

6 NAME OF THE GAME

Meaning: The main purpose or most important aspect of something.

Example: In sales, persistence is the name of the game.

Example: In this business, customer satisfaction is the name of the game.

7 NAME-DROP

Meaning: To mention famous people one knows to impress others.

Example: He likes to name-drop celebrities he's met.

Example: She was name-dropping throughout the conversation.

8 NARROW ESCAPE

Meaning: A situation in which one avoids danger just in time.

Example: He had a narrow escape from the burning building.

Example: She had a narrow escape when her car skidded on ice.

9 NASTY PIECE OF WORK

Meaning: An unpleasant or unkind person.

Example: Be careful of him; he's a nasty piece of work.

Example: She found out too late that her boss was a nasty piece of work.

10 NAVIGATE YOUR WAY THROUGH/TO/AROUND

Meaning: To find a way or manage to move through, reach, or handle a complex situation, location, or task.

Example: She had to navigate her way through the unfamiliar streets of the city to reach the hotel.

Example: He successfully navigated his way to a promotion by handling challenging projects.

11 NEAR DISASTER/COLLAPSE

Meaning: A situation that comes very close to ending in catastrophe or failure.

Example: The company narrowly avoided near collapse by securing emergency funding.

Example: The hikers had a near disaster when they almost fell off the cliff during the storm.

12 NEAR ENOUGH

Meaning: Almost correct or accurate; sufficiently close to the desired result.

Example: The painting isn't perfect, but it's near enough to what I imagined.

Example: The instructions weren't exact, but they were near enough for us to complete the task successfully.

13 NEAR PERFECT

Meaning: Almost flawless or ideal; extremely close to being perfect.

Example: Her performance in the competition was near perfect, earning her a standing ovation.

Example: The design of the new gadget is near perfect, with only minor adjustments needed.

14 NECESSITY IS THE MOTHER OF INVENTION

Meaning: Difficult situations inspire creative solutions or innovative ideas.

Example: During the power outage, they invented a way to cook using a makeshift stove—necessity is the mother of invention.

Example: When the team ran out of resources, they developed a clever alternative because necessity is the mother of invention.

15 NECK AND NECK

Meaning: Very close in a race or competition.

Example: The two runners were neck and neck in the final stretch.

Example: The election results were neck and neck.

16 NEED I ASK?/ NEED I SAY MORE?/ NEED I GO ON?

Meaning: A rhetorical question to emphasize that something is obvious or does not need further explanation.

Example: He constantly shows up late and never finishes his tasks—need I say more?

Example: She's been the top performer for three years in a row—need I ask why she got the promotion?

17 NEEDLE IN A HAYSTACK

Meaning: Something that is very difficult to find.

Example: Finding the lost ring in the field was like looking for a needle in a haystack.

Example: Searching for the file in the cluttered office was like finding a needle in a haystack.

18 NEEDLE SOMEONE

Meaning: To irritate or provoke someone.

Example: He loves to needle his younger brother.

Example: She was needling him about his mistake all day.

19 NEEDLESS TO SAY

Meaning: Used to indicate that what follows is obvious or understood without being stated.

Example: Needless to say, she was thrilled when she got the job offer.

Example: The team worked hard all night—needless to say, they were exhausted by morning.

20 NEGOTIATE AN AGREEMENT/CONTRACT

Meaning: To discuss the terms of an agreement or contract to reach a mutually acceptable outcome.

Example: The two companies worked for months to negotiate an agreement that benefited both parties.

Example: She hired a lawyer to help her negotiate the contract with her new employer.

21 NEITHER HERE NOR THERE

Meaning: Not relevant or important.

Example: His opinion is neither here nor there in this matter.

Example: Whether she likes it or not is neither here nor there.

22 NERVOUS EXHAUSTION/STRAIN

Meaning: A state of extreme mental or emotional fatigue caused by prolonged stress or pressure.

Example: After months of working long hours without a break, she began to suffer from nervous exhaustion.

Example: The constant demands of the job put him under severe nervous strain.

23 NEST EGG

Meaning: Savings set aside for the future.

Example: They have a nest egg for their retirement.

Example: He spent years building up his nest egg.

24 NEVER A DULL MOMENT

Meaning: Always something happening or someone entertaining.

Example: With three kids, there's never a dull moment in our house.

Example: Working here, there's never a dull moment.

25 NEVER AGAIN

Meaning: Not at any future time.

Example: After that experience, he vowed never again to travel without insurance.

Example: She promised herself never again to trust him.

26 NEVER EVER

Meaning: Emphatically never; at no time in the past or future.

Example: I will never ever forget what you did for me.

Example: He promised never ever to lie to her again.

27 NEVER FEAR

Meaning: Used to tell someone not to worry.

Example: Never fear; help is on the way.

Example: She said, "Never fear, we will find a solution."

28 NEVER FOR ONE MOMENT

Meaning: Not even for a very short period; never at all.

Example: I never for one moment doubted your honesty.

Example: He never for one moment considered giving up.

29 NEVER LOOK BACK

Meaning: To continue to progress without regret.

Example: After moving to the city, he never looked back.

Example: She started her own business and never looked back.

30 NEVER SAY DIE

Meaning: To never give up; to remain optimistic and persistent.

Example: Even after several rejections, she never says die.

Example: His never-say-die attitude helped him overcome many obstacles.

31 NEVER SAY NEVER

Meaning: One should not say that something is impossible because anything can happen.

Example: "Will you ever move back to your hometown?" "Never say never."

Example: He said he would never try skydiving but never say never

32 NEVER SO MUCH AS

Meaning: Not even to the slightest degree, without doing even the smallest action.

Example: He walked past me without never so much as a glance in my direction.

Example: She left the room and never so much as said goodbye.

33 NEW ARRIVAL

Meaning: A newly arrived person, such as a newborn or new employee.

Example: The family was excited to welcome the new arrival.

Example: The office had a party to celebrate the new arrival in the team.

34 NEW BLOOD

Meaning: New people brought into an organization to introduce fresh ideas.

Example: The company is looking for new blood to invigorate the team.

Example: They hired new blood to bring innovative ideas to the project.

35 NEW BROOM

Meaning: A new person in charge who makes changes and improves things.

Example: The new manager is a new broom, bringing many fresh ideas.

Example: With the new broom in the company, many old practices were changed.

36 NEW HOPE/CONFIDENCE/HOPE

Meaning: A renewed sense of optimism or assurance.

Example: The success of the project gave the team new hope.

Example: She found new confidence in her abilities after the workshop.

37 NEW KID ON THE BLOCK

Meaning: Someone who is new to a place or organization.

Example: He tried to fit in quickly as the new kid on the block.

Example: She was the new kid on the block in the neighborhood.

38 NEW LEASE ON LIFE

Meaning: A renewed and revitalized outlook or purpose.

Example: After the surgery, he felt like he had a new lease on life.

Example: The project gave her a new lease on life.

39 NEW LIFE/DAY/ERA

Meaning: A fresh start or beginning, often implying significant positive change.

Example: Moving to the countryside gave them a new life.

Example: After the storm, it was a new day filled with hope.

Example: The new leadership brought in a new era for the company.

40 NEW MOON

Meaning: The phase of the moon when it is in conjunction with the sun and invisible from Earth, often used to symbolize new beginnings.

Example: Many cultures celebrate the new moon as a time for new beginnings.

Example: The new moon is a perfect time to set new goals.

41 NEXT BIGGEST

Meaning: The second most significant in size, importance, or impact.

Example: After the capital, the next biggest city in the country is often the economic hub.

Example: The next biggest challenge for the team is meeting the project deadline.

42 NEXT TO NOTHING

Meaning: Almost nothing; a minimal amount or value.

Example: He worked all summer but earned next to nothing because of the low wages.

Example: The antique was purchased for next to nothing at a yard sale, but it turned out to be very valuable.

43 NICE TRY

Meaning: A phrase used to acknowledge someone's effort, often slightly sarcastic or humorous, when the attempt was unsuccessful.

Example: Nice try, but your excuse isn't convincing enough to skip the meeting.

Example: She guessed the answer wrong, and her teacher smiled, saying, "Nice try, but not quite right."

44 NICK OF TIME

Meaning: Just in time, at the last possible moment.

Example: They arrived in the nick of time to catch the bus.

Example: She finished the project in the nick of time.

45 NAGGING DOUBT/WORRY/SUSPICION

Meaning: A persistent or bothersome feeling of uncertainty, anxiety, or mistrust that is difficult to ignore.

Example: She had a nagging doubt about whether she had locked the door before leaving.

Example: Despite his explanation, a nagging suspicion remained that he wasn't telling the whole truth.

46 NIGHT AND DAY

Meaning: Very different, like night and day.

Example: Their opinions on the matter are like night and day.

Example: The transformation was like night and day.

47 NIGHT OR DAY

Meaning: At any time, whether it is daytime or nighttime, often used to emphasize availability or dedication.

Example: You can call me for help, night or day—I'll always be there.

Example: The store is open for customers, night or day, thanks to their 24/7 service.

48 NIGHT AFTER NIGHT

Meaning: Repeatedly or continuously every night, often implying persistence or monotony.

Example: She stayed up late night after night preparing for her exams.

Example: The baby cried night after night, leaving the parents exhausted.

49 NIGHT OWL

Meaning: A person who stays up late at night.

Example: He's a night owl who works best after midnight.

Example: Being a night owl, she finds it hard to wake up early.

50 NIP IT IN THE BUD

Meaning: To stop something before it becomes a bigger problem.

Example: We need to nip this issue in the bud before it gets worse.

Example: She nipped the conflict in the bud by addressing it early.

Nip it in the bud

51 NINE-DAY WONDER

Meaning: Something that attracts great interest for a short time.

Example: The new gadget was a nine-day wonder.

Example: His fame turned out to be a nine-day wonder.

52 NINETEEN TO THE DOZEN

Meaning: Very fast or energetically, often used to describe someone talking quickly or doing something with great enthusiasm.

Example: She was so excited about the trip that she talked to nineteen to a dozen about all the places she wanted to visit.

Example: He worked nineteen to the dozen to finish the project before the deadline.

53 NO ACCOUNTING FOR TASTE

Meaning: People's preferences are inexplicable.

Example: He loves pineapple on pizza, but there's no accounting for taste.

Example: She likes to wear mismatched socks; there's no accounting for taste.

54 NO-BRAINER

Meaning: Something that is very easy to do or understand.

Example: Choosing the cheaper option was a no-brainer.

Example: The decision to hire her was a no-brainer.

55 NO LOVE LOST

Meaning: Mutual dislike or hatred between two people.

Example: There's no love lost between the two rivals.

Example: It's clear there's no love lost between them.

56 NO-MAN'S LAND

Meaning: An area of uncertainty or unclaimed territory.

Example: The negotiations are in no-man's land at the moment.

Example: The strip of land between the two countries became a no-man's land.

57 NO NEWS IS GOOD NEWS

Meaning: If you hear nothing, it means everything is fine.

Example: We haven't heard from them, but no news is good news.

Example: Sometimes, no news is good news when waiting for test results.

58 NO SPRING CHICKEN

Meaning: Not young anymore.

Example: He's no spring chicken, but he can still play soccer.

Example: She's no spring chicken, but she stays active.

59 NO STRINGS ATTACHED

Meaning: Without any special conditions or restrictions.

Example: They offered him the job with no strings attached.

Example: She gave him the gift with no strings attached.

60 NOD OFF

Meaning: To fall asleep, especially briefly or unintentionally.

Example: He nodded off during the lecture.

Example: She nodded off while watching TV.

61 NONE OTHER THAN SOMEBODY

Meaning: Used to emphasize the surprise or significance of someone mentioned.

Example: The guest speaker was none other than the famous author.

Example: The winner was none other than our local hero.

62 NONE THE WISER

Meaning: Still unaware or lacking understanding about something, even after an explanation or event.

Example: I explained the rules to him twice, but he was none the wiser.

Example: They tried to cover up their mistake, but their boss was none the wiser.

63 NOT A CHANCE

Meaning: Absolutely no possibility.

Example: There is not a chance he would lend her money again.

Example: There's not a chance I'll miss her performance.

64 NOT ALL THERE

Meaning: Not mentally sound or fully aware.

Example: He's acting like he's not all there today.

Example: After the accident, she seemed not all there.

65 NOT BORN YESTERDAY

Meaning: Not easily fooled; experienced.

Example: You can't trick me; I wasn't born yesterday.

Example: She's savvy and wasn't born yesterday.

66 NOT BY A LONG SHOT

Meaning: Not at all; not nearly.

Example: He's not finished with the project, not by a long shot.

Example: They didn't win, not by a long shot.

67 NOT COME NEAR SOMEBODY

Meaning: To be far from equaling or matching someone in ability, quality, or achievement.

Example: Her cooking doesn't come near her grandmother's in taste or presentation.*

Example: His performance didn't come near his usual standard of excellence.

68 NOT FOR ALL THE TEA IN CHINA

Meaning: Not for anything, no matter what is offered.

Example: I wouldn't sell my car, not for all the tea in China.

Example: She wouldn't move back to the city, not for all the tea in China.

69 NOT HAVE A LEG TO STAND ON

Meaning: To have no support or justification for one's argument.

Example: He doesn't have a leg to stand on without evidence.

Example: She realized she didn't have a leg to stand on in the debate.

70 NOT IN A MILLION YEARS

Meaning: Absolutely never.

Example: Not in a million years would I do that.

Example: She wouldn't agree to it, not in a million years.

71 NOT KNOW THE FIRST THING ABOUT

Meaning: To have no knowledge or understanding of something.

Example: He doesn't know the first thing about cooking.

Example: I don't know the first thing about car repair.

72 NOT LIFT A FINGER

Meaning: To not make any effort to help.

Example: He didn't lift a finger to help with the cleaning.

Example: She won't lift a finger if it doesn't benefit her.

73 NOT MINCE WORDS

Meaning: To speak directly and bluntly.

Example: She doesn't mince words when giving feedback.

Example: He minced no words about his disappointment.

74 NOT MY CUP OF TEA

Meaning: Not something one likes or prefers.

Example: Horror movies are not my cup of tea.

Example: Running marathons is not her cup of tea.

75 NOT NEARLY

Meaning: Far from being sufficient, accurate, or close to what is expected or needed.

Example: Our budget is not nearly enough to complete the project.

Example: His explanation was not nearly as detailed as it should have been.

76 NOT NECESSARILY

Meaning: Not always or inevitably; used to indicate that something is not guaranteed or absolute.

Example: Expensive products are not necessarily better than cheaper ones.

Example: Just because he's smiling doesn't necessarily mean he's happy.

77 NOT ON YOUR LIFE

Meaning: Absolutely not; never.

Example: Would I go bungee jumping? Not on your life!

Example: Not on your life will I lend you money again.

78 NOT NOW

Meaning: Used to indicate that the current moment is not a suitable or convenient time for something.

Example: When he tried to start a conversation during her meeting, she said, "Not now, I'm busy."*

Example: "Can we talk about this later? Not now; I have too much on my plate."

79 NOT ONCE

Meaning: Never, not even a single time.

Example: Not once did he complain about the long hours he worked.

Example: She didn't look back, not once, as she walked away.

80 NOT SEE THE FOREST FOR THE TREES

Meaning: To be unable to see the big picture because of focusing on the details.

Example: He's so focused on the details that he can't see the forest for the trees.

Example: Don't get lost in the details and miss the forest for the trees.

81 NOT SIT WELL WITH

Meaning: To not be acceptable or agreeable to someone.

Example: Her decision didn't sit well with the team.

Example: His criticism didn't sit well with her.

82 NOT SOMEONE'S STRONG SUIT

Meaning: Not something someone is good at.

Example: Math is not his strong suit.

Example: Cooking is not my strong suit, but I try.

83 NOT THAT

Meaning: Used to introduce a negative statement that qualifies or makes what was just said less intense.

Example: I enjoy hiking, not that I'm very good at it.

Example: He agreed to the plan, not that he had much of a choice.

84 NOT TO BE SNEEZED AT

Meaning: Not to be dismissed or ignored; valuable or significant.

Example: The pay raise is not to be sneezed at.

Example: The opportunity is not to be sneezed at.

85 NOTHING BUT

Meaning: Only; just.

Example: He wanted nothing but the best for his children.

Example: She had nothing but praise for her team.

86 NOTHING MORE

Meaning: Only this and no additional thing; just this.

Example: She wanted nothing more than to spend time with her family.

Example: He asked for a simple explanation, nothing more.

87 NOTHING OF THE KIND

Meaning: Absolutely not; something completely different.

Example: He claimed to be a doctor but was nothing of the kind.

Example: She expected a fancy dinner, but it was nothing of the kind.

88 NOTHING VENTURED, NOTHING GAINED

Meaning: You can't achieve anything if you don't take risks.

Example: He took a risk because nothing ventured, nothing gained.

Example: She believes in the saying, "Nothing ventured, nothing gained."

89 NOTICEABLE DIFFERENCE/CHANGE/INCREASE

Meaning: A difference, change, or increase that is easily seen, recognized, or detected.

Example: There was a noticeable difference in her confidence after completing the course.*

Example: The company reported a noticeable increase in sales after the new product launch.

90 NOW AND THEN

Meaning: Occasionally; from time to time.

Example: We go out for dinner now and then.

Example: He visits his hometown now and then.

91 NOW THEN

Meaning: A phrase used to draw attention, start a conversation, or change the subject, often in a friendly or authoritative tone.

Example: Now then, let's discuss the plans for the weekend.

Example: Now then, is everyone ready to start the meeting?

92 NOW OR NEVER

Meaning: Something must be done immediately because it might be the last or only opportunity to do it. It often emphasizes the urgency or importance of taking action at that moment.

Example: When the job offer came through, Sarah knew it was *now or never;* she had to decide whether to move to a new city or stay in her comfort zone.

Example: Standing at the edge of the diving board, Jake realized it was now or never if he was ever going to conquer his fear of heights

93 NOW WHAT?

Meaning: Used to ask what should be done next, often implying frustration or confusion.

Example: The computer crashed again. Now what?

Example: We've finished the project. Now what?

94 NOW YOU ARE TALKING

Meaning: Used to express approval or enthusiasm for what someone has just said.

Example: "How about we go out for dinner?" "Now you are talking!"

Example: "Let's take a vacation next month." "Now you are talking!"

95 NOWHERE NEAR

Meaning: Far from being close to something in distance, quality, or amount.

Example: The project is nowhere near finished—we still have weeks of work left.

Example: He's nowhere near as talented as his older brother in playing the piano.

96 NOVEL IDEA/APPROACH

Meaning: A new, original, and innovative concept or method.

Example: She came up with a novel idea to reduce waste by repurposing materials.

Example: The team adopted a novel approach to solving the problem, which was highly effective.

97 NUDGE SOMEBODY TOWARDS SOMETHING

Meaning: To gently encourage or persuade someone to do something.

Example: She nudged her son to study engineering.

Example: The teacher nudged the students towards participating in the science fair.

98 NULL AND VOID

Meaning: Having no legal force; invalid.

Example: The contract was declared null and void.

Example: The agreement is null and void after the deadline.

99 NUTS AND BOLTS

Meaning: The primary, practical details of a task or situation.

Example: He explained the nuts and bolts of the project.

Example: Let's focus on the nuts and bolts of the plan.

100 NUMBER CRUNCHER

Meaning: Someone good with numbers, often an accountant or analyst.

Example: She's the best number cruncher in the finance department.

Example: The company hired a number cruncher to sort out their accounts.

* * *

ACTIVITY 6

Please fill in the blanks with the idioms in italics

Nina _____1_____ when it came to her studies. She was determined to graduate at the top of her class; nothing would distract her from her goal. But when her best friend_____2_____ a weekend getaway, Nina felt like she needed to let her hair down for once.

They drove to a secluded cabin in the mountains, where Nina could finally relax. It was _____3_____—a chance to unwind before the final exams. As they hiked through the forest, Nina couldn't help but feel that this trip was a _____4_____. She realized that sometimes, taking care of yourself is _____5_____.

Back at school, Nina felt refreshed and more focused than ever. Her friends noticed the difference and asked what her secret was. "Sometimes, you just have to _____6_____ before it gets out of hand," she replied with a smile. With her new outlook, Nina knew she would finish the semester strong and _____7_____.

* * *

never says die

nudged her towards

now or never

new lease on life

not to be sneezed at.

nip stress in the bud

never look back

A RECAP OF IDIOMS LEARNT: CAN YOU GUESS THE MEANING OF THESE SENTENCES?

- She hit the nail on the head during the meeting, making sure to leave no stone unturned in her explanation.
- Losing his business was the nail in his coffin. He tried to be upbeat about it, but it felt like searching for a needle in a haystack, looking for light at the end of the tunnel.

Is this easy? Or are you feeling overwhelmed? One-on-one training is available. For more information, see the Afterword at the end of the book.

IDIOMS BEGINNING WITH O

$\mathcal{H}$ ere's the 100

1 OFF AND ON

Meaning: Intermittently; happening occasionally rather than continuously.

Example: It rained off and on throughout the afternoon.

Example: He has been working on his novel off and on for years.

2 OFF BASE

Meaning: Incorrect or mistaken.

Example: His assumptions were way off base.

Example: You're off base if you think she'll forgive you easily.

3 OFF ONE'S ROCKER

Meaning: Crazy or insane.

Example: Anyone who thinks that's a good idea is off their rocker.

Example: She must be off her rocker to spend that much money on a dress.

4 OFF THE BEATEN PATH

Meaning: In an isolated or unusual place.

Example: They prefer to travel to destinations that are off the beaten path.

Example: The restaurant is off the beaten path but worth the drive.

5 OFF THE CUFF

Meaning: Without preparation or planning.

Example: He gave a speech off the cuff at the award ceremony.

Example: Her remarks during the meeting were off the cuff.

6 OFF THE HOOK

Meaning: Free from blame or responsibility.

Example: The teacher let him off the hook for not doing his homework.

Example: Thanks for helping me; now I'm off the hook.

7 OFF THE MARK

Meaning: Not accurate or correct.

Example: His predictions were off the mark.

Example: Her guess was way off the mark.

8 OFF THE RADAR

Meaning: Not receiving attention or in the public eye.

Example: The issue has been off the radar for a while.

Example: The artist has been off the radar, working on a new project.

9 OFF THE RAILS

Meaning: Out of control.

Example: The project went off the rails after the team lost funding.

Example: His behavior has been off the rails lately.

10 OFF THE RECORD

Meaning: Information not intended for official publication or disclosure.

Example: He told the journalist something off the record.

Example: Can I tell you something off the record?

11 OFF THE TOP OF ONE'S HEAD

Meaning: Without careful thought or investigation.

Example: I can't think of any solutions off the top of my head.

Example: Off the top of my head, I would suggest calling customer service.

12 OFF THE WALL

Meaning: Unusual or unconventional.

Example: His ideas are often off the wall but sometimes brilliant.

Example: That was an off-the-wall suggestion, but it just might work.

13 OLD HAND

Meaning: Someone experienced in a particular activity.

Example: He's an old hand at carpentry.

Example: She sought advice from an old hand in the industry.

14 ON A ROLL

Meaning: Experiencing a period of success or good luck.

Example: He's been on a roll since he started his new job.

Example: The team is on a roll, winning their last five games.

15 ON A SHOESTRING

Meaning: With a very small amount of money.

Example: They started the business on a shoestring.

Example: She managed to travel the world on a shoestring budget.

16 ON BORROWED TIME

Meaning: Living or existing in a temporary state, usually facing an impending end.

Example: The old car is running on borrowed time.

Example: After the accident, he felt like he was living on borrowed time.

17 ON CLOUD NINE

Meaning: Extremely happy.

Example: He was on cloud nine after winning the lottery.

Example: She felt like she was on cloud nine when she got the promotion.

18 ON EDGE

Meaning: Nervous or tense.

Example: He's been on edge since the accident.

Example: She felt on edge waiting for the exam results.

19 ON PINS AND NEEDLES

Meaning: Anxiously waiting for something.

Example: They were on pins and needles waiting for the news.

Example: She was on pins and needles during the job interview.

20 ON THE BALL

Meaning: Alert and quick to respond or understand.

Example: She's really on the ball and always completes her work on time.

Example: The new manager is on the ball, quickly addressing issues.

21 ON THE BLINK

Meaning: Not working properly.

Example: My computer is on the blink again.

Example: The refrigerator is on the blink and needs to be repaired.

22 ON THE DOT

Meaning: Exactly on time.

Example: She arrived at the meeting on the dot.

Example: The train left at 5 p.m. on the dot.

23 ON THE DOUBLE

Meaning: Immediately; very quickly.

Example: The boss wants this report on the double.

Example: He finished the task on the double.

24 ON THE FENCE

Meaning: Undecided or unsure about something.

Example: He's still on the fence about which college to attend.

Example: She's on the fence about accepting the job offer.

25 ON THE FLY

Meaning: While in motion or progress, without stopping.

Example: She made the decision on the fly.

Example: He prepared his speech on the fly.

26 ON THE GO

Meaning: Hectic; constantly moving or active.

Example: She's always on the go, juggling work and family.

Example: He's been on the go with meetings and errands all day.

27 ON THE HOUSE

Meaning: Free; paid for by the establishment.

Example: The drinks were on the house to celebrate the opening.

Example: The restaurant offered dessert on the house.

28 ON THE LEVEL

Meaning: Honest and sincere.

Example: He seems to be on the level about his intentions.

Example: She wanted to be sure the deal was on the level.

29 ON THE LINE

Meaning: At risk.

Example: His reputation is on the line with this project.

Example: They put everything on the line for their new business.

30 ON THE MEND

Meaning: Recovering from an illness or injury.

Example: He's been in the hospital but is now on the mend.

Example: Their finances are finally on the mend after a rough year.

31 ON THE MONEY

Meaning: Exactly right; accurate.

Example: Her prediction was right on the money.

Example: The budget estimate was on the money.

32 ON THE NOSE

Meaning: Exactly correct; precise.

Example: He arrived at 8 a.m. on the nose.

Example: Her answer was on the nose.

33 ON THE RISE

Meaning: Increasing in popularity or occurrence.

Example: Crime rates are on the rise in the city.

Example: The new singer's popularity is on the rise.

34 ON THE RIGHT TRACK

Meaning: Following a course that is likely to lead to success.

Example: The team is on the right track with their new strategy.

Example: His recent improvements show that he's on the right track

35 ON THE ROCKS

Meaning: In a state of difficulty or trouble.

Example: Their marriage is on the rocks.

Example: The company's finances are on the rocks.

36 ON THE SAME PAGE

Meaning: In agreement; having a shared understanding.

Example: Let's ensure we're all on the same page before starting.

Example: The team needs to be on the same page.

37 ON THE SPOT

Meaning: Immediately; at that moment.

Example: He was hired on the spot after the interview.

Example: She was put on the spot with a difficult question.

38 ON THE TABLE

Meaning: Available for consideration or discussion.

Example: All options for solving the problem are on the table.

Example: The offer is still on the table.

39 ON THE TIP OF ONE'S TONGUE

Meaning: Almost able to be remembered or recalled.

Example: Her name is on the tip of my tongue, but I can't remember it.

Example: The answer was on the tip of his tongue.

40 ON THE UP AND UP

Meaning: Honest and trustworthy.

Example: The deal seems to be on the up and up.

Example: He's a politician who's on the up and up.

42 ON THIN ICE

Meaning: In a risky or precarious situation.

Example: He's on thin ice after missing another deadline.

Example: She's on thin ice with her boss due to her repeated mistakes.

43 ONCE A ..., ALWAYS A ...

Meaning: Suggests that once someone has been something, they will always remain that way.

Example: Once a teacher, always a teacher; she couldn't resist helping the students.

Example: Once a scout, always a scout; he still follows the scout's code of conduct.

44 ONCE BITTEN, TWICE SHY

Meaning: After having a bad experience, one is cautious in the future.

Example: He was cheated once, and now he's once bitten, twice shy.

Example: After the car accident, she's once bitten, twice shy about driving in the rain.

45 ONCE IN A BLUE MOON

Meaning: Very rarely.

Example: She visits her hometown once in a blue moon.

Example: He only goes to the movies once in a blue moon.

46 ONCE IN A LIFETIME

Meaning: Very rare or unique; happening only once in one's life.

Example: The opportunity to travel to Antarctica is a once in a lifetime experience.

Example: Winning the lottery was a once in a lifetime event.

47 ONCE IN A WHILE

Meaning: Occasionally; not often.

Example: We go out for dinner once in a while.

Example: Once in a while, he takes a break from his busy schedule.

48 ONCE IS ENOUGH

Meaning: One experience is sufficient, often because it was unpleasant.

Example: I went skydiving once, and once is enough.

Example: Eating that spicy dish once is enough for me.

49 ONCE OR TWICE

Meaning: A few times.

Example: I've only been to that restaurant once or twice.

Example: She called me once or twice to check on the progress.

50 ONE AFTER ANOTHER

Meaning: Sequentially; one following another in a series.

Example: The cars passed by one after another.

Example: The children took turns on the slide one after another.

51 ONE AND ALL

Meaning: Everyone; all people.

Example: The invitation was extended to one and all.

Example: One and all are welcome to join the celebration.

52 ONE AND THE SAME

Meaning: Exactly the same person or thing.

Example: The two documents were one and the same.

Example: He discovered that the author and the speaker were one and the same.

53 ONE FOR THE BOOKS

Meaning: Something remarkable or noteworthy.

Example: Their wedding was one for the books.

Example: The game was definitely one for the books.

54 ONE IN A MILLION

Meaning: Very rare or unique.

Example: She's one in a million, a truly special person.

Example: Finding a job like this is one in a million.

55 OPEN A CAN OF WORMS

Meaning: To create a complicated situation by starting something.

Example: Discussing politics at dinner opened a can of worms.

Example: Be careful with that topic; it might open a can of worms.

56 OPEN A NEW CHAPTER

Meaning: To start a new phase or period in one's life, often involving significant changes or new experiences. It suggests moving forward from the past and embracing new opportunities or challenges.

Example: After graduating from college, Jenna decided to open a new chapter by moving to a different city and starting her first job.

Example: Mark was ready to open a new chapter and focus on his passions for travel and photography after selling his business.

57 OPEN BOOK

Meaning: Something or someone that is easy to understand or transparent.

Example: Her life is an open book; she has no secrets.

Example: He's like an open book; you can read his emotions easily.

58 OPEN SECRET

Meaning: Something that is supposed to be a secret but is known by many people.

Example: Their relationship was an open secret in the office.

Example: It's an open secret that he's planning to retire soon.

59 OPEN SOMEBODY'S EYES TO SOMETHING

Meaning: To make someone aware of something they were previously unaware of.

Example: The documentary opened her eyes to the effects of climate change.

Example: He opened my eyes to the possibilities of renewable energy.

60 OPEN THE WAY/DOOR TO SOMETHING

Meaning: To create an opportunity for something to happen.

Example: The new law will open the way for more affordable housing.

Example: His promotion opened the door to new career opportunities.

61 OPEN TO SOMETHING

Meaning: Willing to consider or accept something.

Example: She is open to new ideas and suggestions.

Example: He said he was open to discussing the issue further.

62 OPEN YOUR HEART

Meaning: To share your true feelings or thoughts with someone.

Example: She opened her heart to him about her past.

Example: He opened his heart during the therapy session.

63 OPEN YOUR MIND

Meaning: To be willing to consider or accept new ideas, opinions, or perspectives.

Example: Traveling to different countries can help you open your mind to new cultures and ways of living.

Example: She encouraged her students to open their minds and think critically about the subject.

64 OPPORTUNITY TO DO SOMETHING

Meaning: A chance to do something.

Example: She had the opportunity to travel abroad for work.

Example: He took the opportunity to learn a new skill.

65 OPPOSITES ATTRACT

Meaning: The idea that people who are very different from each other are often attracted to each other.

Example: They are a classic case of opposites attract; he's quiet, and she's outgoing.

Example: The saying "opposites attract" applies perfectly to their relationship.

66 OPTION OF DOING SOMETHING

Meaning: The possibility or choice to do something.

Example: She had the option of working from home.

Example: They gave us the option of staying an extra night at the hotel.

67 OR RATHER

Meaning: Used to correct oneself or to introduce a more precise statement.

Example: The meeting is at 3 p.m., or rather, it starts at 3:30 p.m.

Example: He was tired, or rather, exhausted after the trip.

68 ORIENT YOURSELF

Meaning: To find your position or direction, either physically in a location or mentally in a situation.

Example: She stopped to orient herself with the map before continuing the hike.

Example: It took him a while to orient himself to the new job and its responsibilities.

69 OSTENSIBLE REASON/PURPOSE/AIM

Meaning: The apparent or stated reason, purpose, or aim, which may not be the real one.

Example: His ostensible reason for the trip was business, but he also wanted to visit his family.

Example: The ostensible purpose of the meeting was to discuss the budget, but it turned into a policy debate.

70 OTHER THAN

Meaning: Except for; in addition to.

Example: Other than the weather, the trip was perfect.*

Example: She has no hobbies other than reading and painting.

71 OUT IN THE OPEN

Meaning: Revealed or public.

Example: They decided to bring their relationship out in the open.

Example: The discussion brought many issues out in the open.

72 OUT OF BOUNDS

Meaning: Beyond the acceptable or allowed limits.

Example: That topic is out of bounds during the meeting.

Example: The ball was out of bounds, so the play was stopped.

73 OUT OF GAS

Meaning: Exhausted; out of energy.

Example: After running the marathon, she was completely out of gas.

Example: He looked out of gas after working all night.

74 OUT OF LINE

Meaning: Inappropriate or improper behavior.

Example: His comments were out of line and offensive.

Example: She was reprimanded for stepping out of line.

75 OUT OF ONE'S DEPTH

Meaning: In a situation that is beyond one's abilities or knowledge.

Example: He felt out of his depth in the advanced math class.

Example: She was out of her depth when discussing complex legal issues.

76 OUT OF ONE'S ELEMENT

Meaning: In an unfamiliar or uncomfortable situation.

Example: He felt out of his element at the fancy dinner party.

Example: She was out of her element in the new job.

77 OUT OF ORDER

Meaning: Not working properly; broken.

Example: The vending machine is out of order.

Example: The elevator was out of order, so we had to use the stairs.

78 OUT OF POCKET

Meaning: Expenses paid with one's own money; not covered by insurance.

Example: The repairs cost him a lot out of pocket.

Example: She had to pay for the medication out of pocket.

79 OUT OF SIGHT

Meaning: Hidden or not visible.

Example: The kids hid out of sight when they played hide and seek.

Example: He kept his valuables out of sight.

80 OUT OF SIGHT, OUT OF MIND

Meaning: Forgotten when not seen or present.

Example: Once he moved away, he was out of sight, out of mind.

Example: The broken toy was out of sight, out of mind for the child.

81 OUT OF SORTS

Meaning: Feeling slightly unwell, upset, or not in a good mood.

Example: He's been out of sorts since he caught a cold last week.*

Example: She seemed out of sorts after hearing the disappointing news.

82 OUT OF THE BLUE

Meaning: Suddenly and unexpectedly.

Example: He called me out of the blue after years of no contact.

Example: The storm came out of the blue.

83 OUT OF THE LOOP

Meaning: Not informed or included in a particular group or activity.

Example: I feel out of the loop since I missed the last meeting.

Example: He was out of the loop on the latest developments.

84 OUT OF THE ORDINARY

Meaning: Unusual; not normal.

Example: Her behavior was out of the ordinary today.

Example: They experienced something out of the ordinary during their trip.

85 OUT OF THE QUESTION

Meaning: Not possible or allowed.

Example: Taking a vacation now is out of the question.

Example: Selling the house is out of the question.

86 OUT OF THE RUNNING

Meaning: No longer being considered; eliminated from competition.

Example: She's out of the running for the promotion.

Example: Their team is out of the running for the championship.

87 OUT OF THE WAY

Meaning: In a remote or inconvenient location.

Example: The cabin is out of the way but very peaceful.

Example: The restaurant is a bit out of the way, but the food is worth it.

88 OUT OF THE WOODS

Meaning: Out of danger or difficulty.

Example: He's still in the hospital but out of the woods.

Example: Their financial situation is improving, but they're not out of the woods yet.

89 OUT OF THIS WORLD

Meaning: Extremely good, impressive, or amazing.

Example: The chocolate cake she baked was out of this world.

Example: Their performance at the concert was out of this world.

90 OUT OF YOUR MIND

Meaning: To be crazy, irrational, or extremely foolish; also used to describe being overwhelmed or consumed by strong emotions.

Example: You must be out of your mind to drive in this storm.

Example: She was out of her mind with worry when her son didn't come home on time.

91 OUT ON A LIMB

Meaning: In a risky or precarious position.

Example: He went out on a limb to support the new policy.

Example: She's out on a limb with her unconventional ideas.

92 OUTSIDE OF SOMETHING

Meaning: Beyond the limits, scope, or involvement of someone or something; in addition to.

Example: Outside of his work, he has very little time for hobbies.

Example: This matter falls outside of my area of expertise.

93 OVER ONE'S HEAD

Meaning: Beyond one's ability to understand or deal with.

Example: The math problem was over his head.

Example: She felt the new responsibilities were over her head.

94 OVER THE HILL

Meaning: Past one's prime; too old.

Example: He jokes that he's over the hill now that he's turned 50.

Example: Some people think she's over the hill but still very active.

95 OVER THE HUMP

Meaning: Past the most challenging part of something.

Example: Once we're over the hump, the project will be easier to complete.

Example: She's finally over the hump with her recovery.

96 OVER THE LONG HAUL

Meaning: Over a long period of time.

Example: The investment will pay off over the long haul.

Example: He's committed to the project over the long haul.

97 OVER THE MOON

Meaning: Extremely happy or delighted.

Example: She was over the moon about her new job.

Example: He was over the moon when his team won the championship.

Over the moon

98 OVER THE TOP

Meaning: Excessive or exaggerated.

Example: The decorations for the party were over the top.

Example: His reaction was a bit over the top.

99 OVER TO SOMEBODY

Meaning: To pass control, responsibility, or attention to someone else.

Example: After presenting her part, she handed it over to her colleague to continue the discussion.*

Example: The host said, "Now, over to you for the weather update."

100 OWN UP TO

Meaning: To admit or confess to something.

Example: He finally owned up to breaking the vase.

Example: She owned up to her mistakes during the meeting.

.

* * *

ACTIVITY 7

Please fill in the blanks with the idioms in italics given below:

Olivia had always been _____1_____ about any new adventure that came her way. When she got the offer to work abroad, she jumped at the opportunity, even though it meant moving to a place where she didn't know a soul. "It's a chance to _____2_____ in my life," she thought, feeling both excited and nervous.

Her first few weeks in the new country were overwhelming. The language barrier and cultural differences often made her feel like she was _____3_____. But for Olivia it was_____4_____ to give up.

_____5_____, after a particularly challenging meeting, Olivia received an email from her boss praising her efforts. "Looks like I'm _____6_____

" she thought with relief. Slowly but surely, things started falling into place. She had the _____7_____ new friends and picked up the language.

* * *

on the ball

open a new chapter

out of her depth

out of the question

Out of the blue

on the right track,

opportunity to make

A RECAP OF IDIOMS LEARNT: CAN YOU GUESS AT THE MEANING OF THESE SENTENCES?

- She kept her opinions to herself, knowing it was best not to open a can of worms in the meeting.
- He was quick to strike when the opportunity knocked, knowing it doesn't come around often.

You can find out where you stand on idiomatic expressions in the Afterword at the end of this book.

IDIOMS BEGINNING WITH P

*H*ere's the 100

1 PACK IT IN

Meaning: To stop doing something, especially a job.

Example: He decided to pack it in and retire early.

Example: After years of working in the industry, she packed it in and moved to the countryside.

2 PACK OF LIES

Meaning: A completely false story or statement.

Example: Everything he said was a pack of lies.

Example: The article turned out to be a pack of lies.

3 PACK SOMEBODY IN

Meaning: To attract a large number of people.

Example: The new movie packed them in on opening night.

Example: The concert packed with thousands of fans

4 PACK YOUR BAGS

Meaning: To prepare for departure, often suddenly.

Example: He was told to pack his bags and leave immediately.

Example: We need to pack our bags for the weekend trip.

5 PAINT THE TOWN RED

Meaning: To go out and have a lively, enjoyable time.

Example: They decided to paint the town red to celebrate the win.

Example: Let's paint the town red this weekend!

paint the town red

6 PAINFULLY AWARE

Meaning: Very conscious of something.

Example: She is painfully aware of her limitations.

Example: He was painfully aware of the awkward silence.

7 PAMPER YOURSELF

Meaning: To treat yourself luxuriously.

Example: She decided to pamper herself with a spa day.

Example: He pampers himself with gourmet meals.

8 PANDER TO YOUR EVERY WHIM

Meaning: To indulge someone's every desire or wish.

Example: He panders to her every whim, no matter how unreasonable.

Example: The hotel staff pandered to their every whim.

9 PANDORA'S BOX

Meaning: A source of extensive unforeseen problems.

Example: Introducing the new law opened a Pandora's box of issues.

Example: Discussing politics at dinner opened a Pandora's box.

10 PANIC BUYING/SELLING

Meaning: Buying or selling goods or stocks quickly and in large amounts due to fear.

Example: There was panic buying at the supermarket before the storm.

Example: Panic selling caused the stock market to crash.

11 PARADE AS SOMETHING/BE PARADED AS SOMETHING

Meaning: To present or display someone or something in a way that may not be accurate.

Example: He paraded as an expert but had no real qualifications.

Example: She was paraded as the new face of the company.

12 PARK YOURSELF

Meaning: To sit down or settle in a specific spot, often in a casual or relaxed manner.

Example: Why don't you park yourself on the couch while I grab us some drinks?

Example: He parked himself by the window and started reading his book.

13 PART AND PARCEL OF SOMETHING

Meaning: An essential or integral component of something; something that cannot be separated from the whole.

Example: Hard work is part and parcel of achieving success in life.

Example: Dealing with criticism is part and parcel of being a public figure.

14 PART COMPANY

Meaning: To separate or end a relationship, association, or agreement with someone or something.

Example: After years of working together, they decided to part company and pursue individual projects.

Example: The band parted company with their manager over creative differences.

15 PART OF ME/HIM/HER

Meaning: Used to express a conflicted feeling or thought.

Example: Part of me wants to stay, but part of me wants to go.

Example: Part of him felt guilty, but part of him felt relieved.

16 PARTING SHOT

Meaning: A final remark, often critical or cutting, made as one leaves or concludes.

Example: He delivered a parting shot about the team's poor leadership as he left the meeting.

Example: Her parting shot was a sarcastic comment about his inability to meet deadlines.

17 PASS BY

Meaning: To go past or move near something or someone without stopping or to let an opportunity go without taking advantage of it.

Example: I saw an old friend pass by the café, but I didn't have time to say hello.

Example: Don't let this chance pass by; it might not come again!

18 PASS DOWN

Meaning: To hand something from one person or generation to the next.

Example: The family recipe has been passed down for generations.

Example: She plans to pass down her grandmother's jewelry to her daughter.

19 PASS SOMEBODY OFF AS SOMETHING

Meaning: To pretend that someone or something is something they are not, often to deceive others.

Example: He tried to pass himself off as a lawyer, but he didn't have any legal training.

Example: They passed the fake painting off as an original masterpiece.

20 PASS SOMEBODY OVER

Meaning: To overlook or ignore someone, often in the context of promotions or opportunities.

Example: She was upset when she was passed over for a promotion despite her hard work.

Example: They passed him over for the project and chose someone with more experience.

21 PASS SOMETHING TO SOMEBODY

Meaning: To give, hand, or transfer something to another person.

Example: Can you pass the salt to me, please?

Example: He passed the documents to his colleague during the meeting.

22 PASS THE BUCK

Meaning: To shift responsibility to someone else.

Example: He always tries to pass the buck when something goes wrong.

Example: The manager refused to pass the buck and took responsibility.

24 PASS UP THE OPPORTUNITY/CHANCE/OFFER

Meaning: To decline or fail to take advantage of something.

Example: He passed up a chance to study abroad.

Example: She didn't want to pass up the opportunity to work with a famous director.

Example: They passed up the offer because it wasn't what they were looking for.

25 PASS WITH FLYING COLORS

Meaning: To succeed brilliantly or achieve high marks.

Example: She passed the exam with flying colors.

Example: He passed the interview with flying colors.

26 PASSED OFF WELL

Meaning: To be successful or to be received positively.

Example: The event passed off well, with everyone enjoying themselves.

Example: Despite the initial concerns, the presentation passed off well.

27 PASSING INTEREST

Meaning: A temporary or brief interest in something.

Example: He had a passing interest in photography but never pursued it seriously.

Example: Her passing interest in cooking faded after a few weeks.

28 PASSPORT TO SUCCESS

Meaning: Something that guarantees or leads to success.

Example: A good education is often considered a passport to success.

Example: Hard work and dedication are his passport to success.

29 PAT ON THE BACK

Meaning: Praise or recognition for something done well.

Example: She deserves a pat on the back for her hard work.

Example: He got a pat on the back for his excellent presentation.

30 PATH TO FREEDOM/SUCCESS/INDEPENDENCE

Meaning: A course of action that leads to achieving freedom, success, or independence.

Example: Starting his own business was his path to independence.

Example: She believes that education is the path to success.

31 PAVE THE WAY FOR SOMETHING

Meaning: To create the conditions or circumstances for something to happen.

Example: The new legislation will pave the way for significant educational reforms.

Example: Her groundbreaking research paved the way for future discoveries in the field.

32 PAY AN ARM AND A LEG

Meaning: To pay a very high price.

Example: They paid an arm and a leg for their new house.

Example: She paid an arm and a leg for those concert tickets.

33 PAY ATTENTION TO

Meaning: To focus on or take notice of something.

Example: Please pay attention to the instructions before starting the test.

Example: He paid attention to every detail in the report.

34 PAY FOR ITSELF

Meaning: To save enough money to cover the cost of purchase through savings or earnings.

Example: The solar panels will pay for themselves within five years through reduced energy bills.

Example: The investment in the new equipment will pay for itself in increased productivity.

35 PAY SOMEBODY A CALL

Meaning: To visit someone.

Example: She decided to pay her grandmother a call on Sunday.

Example: He paid his old friend a call while he was in town.

36 PAY SOMEBODY BACK FOR SOMETHING

Meaning: To get revenge on someone or return a favor.

Example: She vowed to pay him back for his kindness.

Example: He plans to pay her back for the prank she pulled on him.

37 PAY THE PENALTY/PRICE

Meaning: To suffer the consequences or face the negative results of one's actions.

Example: He paid the penalty for reckless driving with a hefty fine.

Example: She paid the price for her mistakes with a demotion.

38 PAY THE PIPER

Meaning: To face the consequences of one's actions.

Example: Eventually, he had to pay the piper for his mistakes.

Example: They enjoyed themselves but knew they'd have to pay the piper later.

39 PAY THROUGH YOUR NOSE

Meaning: To pay a very high price for something.

Example: They had to pay through the nose for tickets to the concert.

Example: He paid through the nose for that rare collectible.

40 PAY TRIBUTE TO

Meaning: To honor or praise someone or something.

Example: The memorial was built to pay tribute to the fallen soldiers.

Example: She paid tribute to her mentor in her acceptance speech.

41 PAYBACK TIME

Meaning: A moment when someone is rewarded or punished for something they have done, often implying revenge or justice.

Example: After years of hard work, it's finally payback time for her dedication and perseverance.

Example: He was rude to everyone, but it's payback time now that he needs help.

42 PEARLS OF WISDOM

Meaning: Valuable advice or insights that are often shared meaningfully or thoughtfully.

Example: During the meeting, the mentor shared pearls of wisdom about navigating difficult career decisions.

Example: Her grandmother's pearls of wisdom have guided her through many challenging moments in life.

43 PEER TO PEER

Meaning: Direct communication or interaction between individuals of the same status or level.

Example: The software allows for peer-to-peer file sharing.

Example: They had a peer-to-peer discussion about their

44 PENETRATING LOOK/GAZE/EYE

Meaning: A look or gaze that seems to see through someone or something, often conveying intensity, insight, or deep understanding.

Example: She gave him a penetrating look that made him feel as if she knew all his secrets.

Example: His penetrating gaze made everyone in the room fall silent.

45 PENNY PINCHER

Meaning: Someone who is very careful with their money.

Example: He's a real penny pincher and hates spending money.

Example: She has a reputation for being a penny pincher.

46 PEPPER SOMEBODY WITH QUESTIONS

Meaning: To ask someone a large number of questions in quick succession, often overwhelming them.

Example: The reporters peppered the politician with questions about the recent scandal.

Example: The students peppered their teacher with questions about the upcoming exam.

47 PERFECT TIMING

Meaning: The ability to do something at exactly the right moment.

Example: He arrived with the pizzas just as everyone was getting hungry—perfect timing!

Example: Her joke was delivered with perfect timing, making everyone burst into laughter.

48 PERK SOMEBODY UP

Meaning: To make someone feel happier, more energetic, or more alert.

Example: A cup of coffee in the morning always perks me up.

Example: She brought flowers to perk her friend up after a difficult week

49 PERK SOMETHING UP

Meaning: To make something more lively, attractive, or interesting.

Example: Adding a splash of color can really perk up a dull room.

Example: The chef used fresh herbs to perk up the flavor of the soup.

50 PERK UP

Meaning: To become more cheerful, energetic, or lively.

Example: She began to perk up after hearing the good news.

Example: The flowers started to perk up after being watered.

51 PHENOMENAL GROWTH/RISE/INCREASE

Meaning: An exceptionally large or impressive expansion, improvement, or upward change in size, number, or level.

Example: The company experienced phenomenal growth in revenue after launching its new product.

Example: There has been a phenomenal rise in online shopping over the past decade.

52 PICK A QUARREL

Meaning: To deliberately start an argument or disagreement with someone.

Example: He seemed to pick a quarrel with his coworker over the smallest issues.

Example: She was in such a bad mood that she picked a quarrel with her friend over nothing.

53 PICK UP THE PIECES

Meaning: To recover or get back to normal after a setback.

Example: After the disaster, they worked hard to pick up the pieces.

Example: She helped him pick up the pieces after his business failed

54 PICK UP THE TAB

Meaning: To pay the bill or cover the cost of something.

Example: He generously offered to pick up the tab for dinner.

Example: She always picks up the tab when we go out for coffee.

55 PICK SOMEBODY'S BRAIN

Meaning: To ask someone for advice or detailed information about something they know a lot about.

Example: I must pick your brain about the best approach to this project.

Example: She called her mentor to pick his brain about career opportunities in the tech industry.

56 PICK YOURSELF UP

Meaning: To recover from a setback, failure, or difficult situation and move forward.

Example: After losing the match, she rested for a day and then picked herself up to start training again.

Example: Life will knock you down sometimes, but you have to pick yourself up and keep going.

57 PICK UP SPEED

Meaning: To start moving faster or to increase momentum in progress or activity.

Example: The car began to pick up speed as it moved downhill.

Example: The project picked up speed after the team implemented a new strategy.

58 PIERCE SOMEBODY'S HEART

Meaning: To profoundly affect someone emotionally, often causing great pain or sadness.

Example: The tragic news of her friend's passing pierced her heart.

Example: His heartfelt apology pierced her heart, making her realize how much he regretted his actions.

59 PIGS MIGHT FLY

Meaning: Used to indicate that something is extremely unlikely or impossible.

Example: He promised to finish the project on time, but given his track record, pigs might fly.

Example: She promised to quit gossiping, but pigs might fly before that happens.

60 PIG OUT

Meaning: To eat a lot or overeat.

Example: They pigged out on pizza and ice cream.

Example: He tends to pig out during the holidays.

61 PIN DOWN

Meaning: To get a specific commitment or information from someone.

Example: It's hard to pin him down for a meeting.

Example: She managed to pin down the exact date of the event.

62 PINK SLIP

Meaning: A notice of termination from a job.

Example: He received his pink slip yesterday.

Example: Many employees were worried about getting a pink slip.

63 PLAY IT BY EAR

Meaning: To deal with a situation as it develops rather than planning ahead.

Example: Let's just play it by ear and see what happens.

Example: They decided to play it by ear and adjust their plans as needed.

64 PLAY IT SAFE

Meaning: To avoid risk.

Example: He decided to play it safe and take the job offer.

Example: She always plays it safe when it comes to investments.

65 PLAY THE DEVIL'S ADVOCATE

Meaning: To argue the opposite side just for the sake of argument.

Example: He played devil's advocate to test the strength of her argument.

Example: She enjoys playing devil's advocate in discussions.

66 PLAY WITH FIRE

Meaning: To take dangerous risks.

Example: You're playing with fire if you ignore safety regulations.

Example: He knew he was playing with fire by cheating on the test.

67 PLENTY OF FISH IN HE SEA

Meaning: There are many other potential mates or opportunities available.

Example: Don't be upset about the breakup; plenty of fish are in the sea.

Example: She told him that there were plenty of fish in the sea after his failed relationship.

68 POINT A FINGER

Meaning: To blame or accuse someone.

Example: They pointed the finger at him for the mistake.

Example: She didn't want to point the finger without evidence.

69 POKE YOUR NOSE INTO SOMETHING

Meaning: To interfere or get involved in someone else's business or affairs without being invited, often intrusive or unwelcome.

Example: He's always poking his nose into other people's conversations, even when they don't concern him.

Example: I wish my neighbors would stop poking their noses into my personal life. It's really none of their business.

70 POLISH UP SOMETHING

Meaning: To improve or refresh one's knowledge or skills in a particular area. It often refers to revisiting something you have already learned but might need to refine or enhance.

Example: I need to polish up my French before my trip to Paris next month.

Example: He decided to polish up his presentation skills to impress his new clients.

71 POP THE QUESTION

Meaning: To propose marriage.

Example: He popped the question during a romantic dinner.

Example: She had no idea he was going to pop the question.

72 POT CALLING THE KETTLE BLACK

Meaning: Criticizing someone for a fault one also possesses.

Example: Accusing me of being messy is the pot calling the kettle black.

Example: It's a case of the pot calling the kettle black when he complains about her lateness.

73 POUR YOUR/HER/HIS HEART OUT

Meaning: To express one's deepest feelings or thoughts.

Example: She poured her heart out to her best friend.

Example: He poured his heart out in his letter.

Pour one's heart out

74 PRACTICE WHAT YOU PREACH

Meaning: To do what one advises others to do.

Example: He should practice what he preaches about healthy living.

Example: She practices what she preaches when it comes to environmentalism.

75 PRESS/PUSH THE PANIC BUTTON

Meaning: To overreact to a situation.

Example: There's no need to press the panic button; we have everything under control.

Example: She pressed the panic button when she couldn't find her keys.

76 PRIME EXAMPLE

Meaning: To an outstanding or typical instance that clearly illustrates a particular quality, condition, or concept.

Example: The Eiffel Tower is a prime example of French engineering and cultural heritage.

Example: His success in building a profitable business from scratch is a prime example of hard work and perseverance paying off.

77 PRETTY AS A PICTURE

Meaning: Extremely attractive, beautiful, or charming in appearance.

Example: The bride looked as pretty as a picture in her white gown.

Example: The garden in full bloom was as pretty as a picture.

78 PROS AND CONS

Meaning: to the advantages (pros) and disadvantages (cons) of a particular situation or decision. It's often used when weighing the positives and negatives before making a choice.

Example: Before buying a car, consider its pros and cons, such as fuel efficiency versus the cost of maintenance.

Example: Before making her final decision, she made a list of the pros and cons of moving to a new city.

79 PULL A FAST ONE

Meaning: To deceive or trick someone.

Example: He pulled a fast one on his boss by faking the report.

Example: She tried to pull a fast one but got caught.

80 PULL IT OFF

Meaning: To successfully accomplish something complex or unexpected, often despite challenges or doubts from others.

Example: Everyone doubted the team's ability to finish the project on time, but they managed to pull it off and deliver it ahead of schedule.

Example: Despite the complicated recipe, Sarah pulled it off and made a perfect soufflé for the dinner party.

81 PULL ONE'S LEG

Meaning: To joke or tease someone.

Example: Are you pulling my leg, or is this for real?

Example: He loves to pull his sister's leg with silly stories.

82 PULL THE PLUG

Meaning: To stop something; to bring something to an end.

Example: The company pulled the plug on the project due to budget cuts.

Example: She decided to pull the plug on her failing business.

83 PULL THE WOOL OVER ONE'S EYES

Meaning: To deceive or fool someone.

Example: He tried to pull the wool over her eyes with excuses.

Example: Their fake story pulled the wool over everyone's eyes.

84 PUMPED UP

Meaning: To feel very excited, enthusiastic, or energized about something, often in anticipation of an event or activity.

Example: The team was pumped up before the big game, cheering each other on and ready to give their best performance.

Example: After hearing the motivational speech, the employees were pumped up to tackle the new project with renewed energy.

85 PUSHED TO THE LIMIT

Meaning: To be forced to go as far as one can, often to the point of exhaustion, stress, or maximum capacity, either physically, mentally, or emotionally.

Example: During the intense training camp, the athletes were pushed to the limit, testing their endurance and determination.

Example: As the deadline approached, the entire team was pushed to the limit to complete the project on time, working late nights and on weekends.

86 PUT A DAMPER

Meaning: To spoil or lessen the enjoyment of something.

Example: The rain put a damper on the picnic.

Example: His rude comments put a damper on the celebration.

87 PUT ALL YOUR EGGS IN ONE BASKET

Meaning: To risk everything on a single venture.

Example: Investing all your money in one stock is putting all your eggs in one basket.

Example: She put all her eggs in one basket by applying to only one college.

88 PUT DOWN ROOTS

Meaning: To settle and establish a home in a particular place.

Example: They decided to put down roots in the small town.

Example: He put down roots after years of traveling.

89 PUT IN A GOOD WORD

Meaning: To say something positive about someone to help them.

Example: Could you put in a good word for me with your boss?

Example: She put in a good word for him, and he got the job.

90 PUT IN ONE'S PLACE

Meaning: To correct someone's improper behavior.

Example: The teacher put the rude student in his place.

Example: He was put in his place after making that inappropriate comment.

91 PUT MY FINGER ON

Meaning: To identify or pinpoint something.

Example: I can't put my finger on it, but something feels off.

Example: She put her finger on the cause of the problem.

92 PUT ONE'S BEST FOOT FORWARD

Meaning: To make a great effort to make a good impression.

Example: He put his best foot forward at the job interview.

Example: She always puts her best foot forward when meeting new clients.

93 PUT ONE'S CARDS ON THE TABLE

Meaning: To be open and honest about your intentions.

Example: It's time to put our cards on the table and discuss our plans.

Example: He put his cards on the table about his feelings for her.

94 PUT ONE'S FOOT DOWN

Meaning: To be firm or insistent about something.

Example: She put her foot down and refused to let her son go to the party.

Example: The manager put his foot down about meeting deadlines.

95 PUT ONE'S FOOT IN HIS MOUTH

Meaning: To say something embarrassing or inappropriate.

Example: He put his foot in his mouth by making that insensitive joke.

Example: She often puts her foot in her mouth without realizing it.

96 PUT ONE'S MONEY WHERE HIS MOUTH IS

Meaning: To support one's words with actions or financial commitment.

Example: If you believe in the cause, put your money where your mouth is.

Example: He put his money where his mouth is and invested in the project.

97 PUT SOMEBODY ON A PEDESTAL

Meaning: To admire or idealize someone so much that you fail to see their flaws.

Example: She always puts her older brother on a pedestal, thinking he can do no wrong.

Example: It's important not to put celebrities on a pedestal; they're just human like everyone else.

98 PUT THE CART BEFORE THE HORSE

Meaning: To do things in the wrong order.

Example: Planning the celebration before the proposal is putting the cart before the horse.

Example: They were putting the cart before the horse by designing the product before researching the market.

99 PUT TWO AND TWO TOGETHER

Meaning: To figure something out from the information available.

Example: She put two and two together and realized he was lying.

Example: It didn't take long to put two and two together and see what happened.

100 PUT UP A FRONT

Meaning: To pretend to have a certain attitude or emotion.

Example: He put up a front of confidence but was really nervous.

Example: She put up a front to hide her true feelings.

* * *

ACTIVITY 8

Fill in the blanks with the idioms in italics given below.

Paul was known for his persistence; when he set his mind on something, he wouldn't stop until he_____1_____. So when his friends suggested starting a small business together, he thought it was a_____2_____," and Paul quickly realized that starting a business was going to be a lot harder than he thought.

At first, things were rough. They ran into problems _____3_____ marketing mishaps. Paul was _____4_____ that he could run into financial troubles. Still, he refused to panic. He knew that success wasn't just about skill but perseverance.

After months of hard work, they finally started to see progress. Their customer base grew, and the business was beginning to _____5_____. Paul couldn't help but _____6_____. They had been _____7_____, but they had come out stronger on the other side. He realized that sometimes, you have to _____8_____ and trust that things will work out in the end.

As he looked around at their thriving business, Paul knew all the painstaking efforts had been worth it. Hard work and dedication were his _____9_____, and now they were reaping the rewards.

* * *

pulled it off

piece of cake

packed with

painfully aware

pay for itself

pat himself on the back

pushed to the limit

put your cards on the table

passport to success

A RECAP OF IDIOMS LEARNT: CAN YOU GUESS THE MEANING OF THESE SENTENCES?

- If he wanted to lead by example, he had to practice what he preached and implement his plan.
- She was under pressure but managed to pull a rabbit out of the hat and deliver the project on time.

Would you like an opportunity to learn more? Check out the Afterword at the end of this book.

ANSWER KEY TO ACTIVITIES 1 - 8

ACTIVITY 1 IDIOMS BEGINNING WITH I

*I*sabel was **in *over her head*** when she decided to throw a surprise party for her boss. She had always been **in *a tight spot*** trying to get a promotion, but this event was making her *feel ill at ease*. She knew she ***had to impress her boss with a party*** that was amazing, or she would ***incriminate herself.***

The day of the party arrived, and Isabel **was in the driver's seat**, making sure everything was perfect. Just when she thought she could finally take a breath, the cake arrived, and it was ***immediately obvious*** that it was the wrong flavor. "Great," she muttered to herself, "Now I really am ***in a jam.***

Despite the hiccups, the party went off without a hitch. Her boss was thrilled, and Isabel could tell by the end of the night that she was **in her boss' good books**. It seemed her hard work had finally paid off.

* * *

ACTIVITY 2 IDIOMS BEGINNING WITH J

Jordan had always yearned for a life of adventure, so even though he did not have much money. He decided to ***jump off the deep end*** and travel the world. But the journey _**jarred on his nerves**_. He quickly realized that life on the road wasn't as glamorous as he had imagined. He often found himself in _**jam-packed**_ buses, traveling for hours on end with _**just the clothes on his back**_.

During one particularly rough day, Jordan felt like _**jumping ship**_. The rain was pouring, his phone was dead, and he was lost in a foreign city. But then, out of nowhere, a local offered him shelter and a hot meal. "Sometimes," Jordan thought, "you just have to _**jump at the chance**_ when life offers you a bit of kindness."

By the end of his journey, Jordan understood that while his trip was filled with challenges, those hardships had made the experience all the more rewarding. It wasn't always easy, but he was glad he didn't _**jump to conclusions**_ about quitting early.

* * *

ACTIVITY 3 IDIOMS BEGINNING WITH K

Kara was known for being _**keen on doing**_ her work. She always _**knew the ropes**_ for solving problems that others couldn't figure out. But when her company decided to take on a massive project, even Kara felt _**knee-deep in**_ daily problems, hoping everything would go smoothly.

As the deadline approached, Kara started to feel the pressure. She was _**keeping her fingers crossed**_ that the new software they were developing wouldn't have any major glitches. However, just two days before the launch, a critical bug was discovered. Kara knew she had to _**keep her cool**_ and find a solution quickly.

Working late into the night, she managed to _**keep the problem under control**_. The launch was a success, and her boss praised her for her dedication. "You really _**knocked it out of the park**_ this time, Kara," he said with a smile. Kara couldn't help but feel proud. It wasn't easy, but she had _**kept her nose to the grindstone**_ and made it through.

* * *

ACTIVITY 4 IDIOMS BEGINNING WITH L

Lena had always **_looked on the bright side_**, no matter what life threw at her. But when she unexpectedly lost her job, even she found it hard to keep her spirits up. "Sometimes, you just have to **_let the chips fall where they may_**," she told herself, trying to stay positive.

With her savings dwindling, Lena decided it was time to **_learn the ropes_** of freelancing. At first, it was **_like pulling teeth_** —clients were hard to come by, and the competition was fierce. But Lena was determined not to **_lose heart_**. She knew that if she **_lived as there was no tomorrow_** and gave it her all, something good would eventually come her way.

After months of hard work, Lena finally landed a big project. It was **_light at the end of the tunnel_**, and she felt like she was **_living the dream_**. As she signed the contract, she couldn't help but think, "This might have been a tough journey, but I'm glad I didn't **_leave no stone unturned_** in pursuing this new path."

* * *

ACTIVITY 5 IDIOMS BEGINNING WITH M

Max had always been **_a man of few words_**, but when he spoke, people listened. He had a reputation for **_making short work_** when it came to his creative ideas, but that's what made him such a valuable member of the team. His latest project was no different—**_make or break_**, as they called it. The entire company was depending on its success.

Despite the pressure, Max stayed cool as a cucumber. He knew that **_making a mountain out of a molehill_** wouldn't help anyone, so he kept things in perspective and encouraged his team to do the same. They worked morning, noon, and night, there was **_no margin for error_** to prepare everything for the big presentation.

When the day finally arrived, Max took a deep breath and **_made a beeline_** for the conference room. The presentation **_made the grade_**, and the clients were impressed. It was clear that all their hard work had paid off. As they celebrated, Max couldn't help but feel proud. He had **_moved heaven and earth_** to make this happen, and now, he could finally take a moment to relax.

* * *

ACTIVITY 6 IDIOMS BEGINNING WITH N

Nina **_never says die_** when it came to her studies. She was determined to graduate at the top of her class, and nothing was going to distract her from her goal. But when her best friend **_nudged her towards_** a weekend getaway, Nina felt like she needed to let her hair down for once.

They drove to a secluded cabin in the mountains, where Nina could finally relax. It was **_now or never_** —a chance to unwind before the final exams. As they hiked through the forest, Nina couldn't help but feel that this trip was a **_new lease on life_**. She realized that sometimes, taking care of yourself is **_not to be sneezed at_**.

Back at school, Nina felt refreshed and more focused than ever. Her friends noticed the difference and asked what her secret was. "Sometimes, you just have to **_nip stress in the bud_** before it gets out of hand," she replied with a smile. With her new outlook, Nina knew she would finish the semester strong and never look back.

* * *

ACTIVITY 7 IDIOMS BEGINNING WITH O

Olivia had always been **_on the ball_** about any new adventure that came her way. When she got the offer to work abroad, she jumped at the opportunity, even though it meant moving to a place where she didn't know a soul. "It's a chance **_to open a new chapter_** in my life," she thought, feeling both excited and nervous.

Her first few weeks in the new country were overwhelming. The language barrier and cultural differences often made her feel like she was **_out of her depth_**. But for Olivia, it was **_out of the question_** to give up.

Out of the blue, after a particularly challenging meeting, Olivia received an email from her boss praising her efforts. "**_Looks like I'm on the right track_**," she thought with relief. Slowly but surely, things started falling into place. She had the o**_pportunity to make_** new friends, and pick up the language.

* * *

ACTIVITY 8 IDIOMS BEGINNING WITH P

Paul was known for his persistence; when he set his mind on something, he wouldn't stop until he **_pulled it off._** So when his friends suggested starting a small business together, he thought it was a **_piece of cake_** ," and Paul quickly realized that starting a business was going to be a lot harder than he thought.

At first, things were rough. They ran into problems **_packed with_** marketing mishaps. Paul was **_painfully aware_** that he could run into financial troubles. Still, he refused to panic. He knew that success wasn't just about skill—it was about perseverance.

After months of hard work, they finally started to see progress. Their customer base grew, and the business was beginning to **_pay for itself_**. Paul couldn't help but **_pat himself on the back_**. They had been **_pushed to the limit_**, but they had come out stronger on the other side. He realized that sometimes, you have to **_put your cards on the table_** and trust that things will work out in the end.

As he looked around at their thriving business, Paul knew that all the painstaking efforts had been worth it. Hard work and dedication were his **_passport to success_**, and now they were reaping the rewards.

* * *

CONCLUSION

*H*ere are ten tips to help you learn to use idioms effectively in speech:

1 Read Widely: Exposure to idioms through books, articles, and stories helps you understand their context and usage.

2 Watch Proficient Speakers of English: Observe how native speakers use idioms in movies, TV shows, and conversations to see how they naturally fit into dialogue. Try to switch on the English subtitles for the English show you are watching. And try to listen and read the idioms used.

3 Practice with Idiom Lists: Study lists of common idioms and their meanings. Flashcards can be a helpful tool for memorization, and this book is a good help.

4 Learn the Context: Understand the situations in which an idiom is appropriate. Knowing the context helps prevent misuse.

5 Use Idioms in Writing: Incorporate idioms into your writing exercises. This helps reinforce their meanings and proper usage.

6 Speak with Proficicent Speakers of English: Engage in conversations with good speakers who can provide feedback on your use of idioms.

7 Create Sentences: Practice creating your own sentences using new idioms to get comfortable with their structure and meaning.

8 Learn the Origins: Understanding the origin of an idiom can make it easier to remember and use correctly.

9 Daily Practice: Every day, try to use one of the idioms in this book. Unless you actually say it out loud, it becomes a part of your active vocabulary. If you know an idiom but don't use it, it is part of your passive vocabulary and will not make you a proficient speaker of English. So practice using them either in private or with your friends first, so you gain confidence in using them.

10 Be Patient and Consistent: Learning idioms takes time. Regular practice and exposure will gradually improve your ability to use them naturally.

By incorporating these strategies into your language learning routine, you'll become more proficient in using idioms in your speech.

AFTERWORD

Dear Reader

If you feel the need to improve your idiomatic expressions in English and your need to improve pronunciation on a personal level, and you need one-on-one coaching, we do provide coaching lessons via webinars for you. To register your interest, write to A M Lucas at speakeasily123@gmail.com

This coaching will be personalized to your needs.

- 1 call a week for 12 weeks
- I will review your work and help you with your speaking, pronunciation and fluency
- You have access to text message access for a duration of 12 weeks
- Access to all resources that I personally use.

REFERENCES

Pearson Education Limited. (2009). *Longman Dictionary of Contemporary English for Advanced Learners* (5th ed.). Pearson Education Limited.

Seidl, J., & McMordie, W. (2002). *English Idioms* (5th ed.). Oxford University Press.

ABOUT THE AUTHOR

A M Lucas is an author of books on business communication and the English Language . She has written four books on Language Learning.

She has taught writing and speaking skills for 40 years. She has also written a book on pronunciation and three books on idioms.

ALSO BY A M LUCAS

Speaking English Easily: Phonetics for Easy Pronunciation

800 English Idioms from A - H: Master Common Expressions For Fluency And Confident Communication For Intermediate And Advanced Learners

800 English Idioms from I - P: Master Common Expressions For Fluency And Confident Communication For Intermediate And Advanced Learners

800 English Idioms from Q -Z: Master Common Expressions For Fluency And Confident Communication For Intermediate And Advanced Learners

Made in the USA
Las Vegas, NV
11 December 2024

13853194R00115